THE BOOK OF
THATCHAM

THE BOOK OF
THATCHAM
A Record of a Changing Community

PETER ALLEN

HALSGROVE

Dedication
To my wife Ann for sharing my involvement
in the history of our adopted home

British Library Cataloguing-in-Publication Data.
A CIP record for this title is available from the British Library.

ISBN: 1 84114 500 9
ISBN: 978 1 84114 500 6

HALSGROVE

Halsgrove House
Lower Moor Way
Tiverton, Devon EX16 6SS
Tel: 01884 243242
Fax: 01884 243325
E-mail: sales@halsgrove.com
Website: www.halsgrove.com

Frontispiece photograph: *The view north-east of a village soon to become a town –
an aerial view showing Thatcham in 1953. The open spaces and fields seen in and around
its centre will be given up for residential development over the next half-century.*

Printed and bound in Great Britain by CPI, Bath.

CONTENTS

FOREWORD

I consider it to be an honour and a privilege to introduce this very fine local history to you.

Thatcham has been for many years now my adopted professional home, as I am the head teacher of its own large and very successful comprehensive school. I am also privileged to serve the community in a number of other ways. It is these experiences that have emphasised to me the significant way in which modern Thatcham has been shaped by its history and its important role as a growing settlement in this beautiful part of West Berkshire.

It is therefore a great pleasure for me to commend this book to you all and to congratulate the author, Peter Allen, and – on his behalf – to thank all who have made any contribution, however small, towards this magnificent work.

Thatcham has a proud history dating back some 10,000 years. I am sure you will find learning the finer detail of Thatcham's more recent history rewarding and enlightening. Do enjoy this book.

P.G. Dick, OBE JP

President
Thatcham Historical Society

PREFACE

Thatcham's history is relatively well documented today. Over a century ago, Samuel Barfield's research notes were published posthumously in a two-volume history which became the foundation on which later local historical publications built, including the present author's 'popular' paperback history of Thatcham.

My own interest in Thatcham's past emerged from an attempt to make the history lessons I came to teach at the Kennet School a little more relevant to the pupils who first experienced them over 30 years ago. I began collecting material that has now grown into an extensive documentary and photographic archive.

Much of this has already found its way into print in the form of local history books, journal and newspaper articles – not least the column which ran unbroken in the *Thatcham News* for over five years! Nevertheless, it is still appropriate that the present publication should be made available to the inhabitants of Thatcham.

Since Barfield's history of the place was published, Thatcham has changed out of all recognition. It is true to say that developments in the twentieth century have eclipsed those which occurred in earlier times. The village Barfield knew has become a town today and much has happened which should be chronicled.

It is in this spirit that I set about the project suggested by the publisher of this book. *The Book of Thatcham* is intended to be a community history of the place, focusing – in text and pictures – on the changing scene, the emergence of new organisations and the varied lives of the inhabitants during the twentieth century.

In this high quality publication, Thatcham's history is brought into the twenty-first century. I hope the present book may come to be a third volume of Barfield, encapsulating as it does something of Thatcham's twentieth century development – whilst it can never be exhaustive, it does provide a record of a changing community.

Peter Allen
Thatcham, 2006

'Everything changes and everything stays the same' – seven decades apart, these two views show the view south into Thatcham's Broadway in 1915 and 1985.

A TIMELINE OF THATCHAM

c.8,400–c.7,500BC	Mesolithic (Stone Age) settlement (Thatcham Moors)
c.1,500BC	Bronze Age settlement (Dunston Park)
c.500BC	Iron Age settlement (Dunston Park)
c.250–375AD	Romano-British settlement (Thatcham Newtown)
c.500AD	Saxon Chief Tace establishes his village (?)
c.675	Saxon church is built at Thatcham
c.971	Thatcham becomes a Royal Manor
1086	Thatcham Hundred comprises 17 manors
1121	Reading Abbey is founded by Henry I
1123	Thatcham becomes a Monastic Manor
c.1141	A Norman church is built at Thatcham
c.1160	Thatcham market is attacked by Newbury men
1218	Market day is changed from Sunday to Thursday
1222	Thatcham is granted a two-day annual fair
c.1300	Thatcham becomes a Borough
1304	The Chapel of the Borough is built
1306	Thatcham is first taxed as a Borough
1316	The vicarage of Thatcham is instituted
1348–9	The Black Death decimates the local population
c.1430	Thomas Loundyes' Charity is established
c.1520	The Danvers' Chapel is added to the Parish Church
1539	Reading Abbey is dissolved by Henry VIII
c.1540	John Winchcombe becomes Lord of the Manor
c.1590	John Hunt's Charity is established
1707	Lady Frances Winchcombe's school is established
1718	Thatcham Manor becomes forfeit to the Crown
c.1720	Turnpike Road (Theale–Speen) is opened
1722	Brigadier-General Waring becomes Lord of the Manor
1722	Dunston House is built
1723	Kennet Navigation (Reading–Newbury) is opened
1795	Speenhamland System of Poor Relief is instituted
1798	Dunston House is demolished
1800	Food riots occur in and around Thatcham
1802	William Mount becomes Lord of the Manor
1804	Independent chapel in Church Lane is opened
1810	Kennet and Avon Canal (Newbury–Bath) is opened
1811	Thatcham's first Enclosure Act is passed
c.1815	Stephen Pinnock's woodturnery works is opened
1828	First National School (Broadway) is opened
1830	Machine riots occur in and around Thatcham
1834	Wesleyan Methodist chapel is opened
1839	Thatcham Agricultural Society is founded
1840	Primitive Methodist chapel is opened
1844	Francis Baily is buried in the Parish Church
1846	National School (Park Lane) is opened
1847	British School (Church Lane) is opened
1847	Berks and Hants Railway (Reading–Hungerford) is opened
1849	Thatcham's second Enclosure Act is passed
1861	John Henry takes over Colthrop Mill
1866	Thatcham gas works is established
1879	Thatcham Cottage Garden Society is founded
1880	Thatcham sewage works is established

1895	Inaugural meeting of Thatcham Parish Council
1896	Newbury sewage works (in Thatcham) is constructed
1900	Thatcham Nursing Society is founded
1902	William House is awarded the VC
1905	Thatcham's police station is opened
1906	GWR line to West Country is completed
1907	The Parish Hall is built
1911	A.H. & C.G. Brown's motor works is founded
1911	Tomlin memorial fountain and shelter is erected
1912	First public telephone is installed in Thatcham
1913	Council School (Francis Baily) is opened
1915	Alexander Buller Turner is awarded the VC
1918	Cropper & Company take over Colthrop Mill
1920	Thatcham electric light works is established
1920	Thatcham's war memorial is dedicated
1921	Thatcham Road Transport Services is founded
1928	Local roads are officially named and numbered
1931	Mains water is supplied (from Cold Ash reservoir)
1935	First Thatcham Scouts established
1938	Thatcham Women's Voluntary Service founded
1938	Thatcham Women's Institute is founded
1940	The Army depot in Station Road is opened
1942	Victor Buller Turner is awarded the VC
1947	Memorial Playing-field comes into use
1957	Kennet Secondary School is opened
1958	Brown's (Broadway) woodturnery works closes down
1962	High Street relief road is completed
1964	St Mary's (Park Lane) Primary School is opened
1964	St Mary's (Broadway) Infant School is closed
1965	Thatcham's station buildings demolished/unstaffed
1969	Thatcham's police station is closed
1972	Whitelands Park and Parsons Downs schools open
1974	Thatcham Parish Council becomes a Town Council
1978	Thatcham Health Centre is opened
1978	Thatcham Catholic church is opened
1980	The (original) Children's Centre is opened
1981	New public library (Walnut Close) is opened
1983	Thatcham's police station reopens (part-time)
1985	Colthrop South Board Mill closed
1986	Kingsland shopping centre comes into use
1987	New Thatcham Station is opened/staffed
1987	Thatcham Baptist church is opened
1988	Kennet sports centre is opened to the public
1989	Spurcroft Primary School is officially opened
1990	New John Hunt Almshouse opened
1990	Kennet and Avon Canal reopened throughout
1992	Thatcham Football Club move to Waterside Park
1995	Thatcham Nature Discovery Centre opened
1996	Henwick Worthy sports ground comes into use
1999	Northern distributor road is completed
2000	Thatcham North Board Mill Closed
2000	The Army depot in Station Road is closed

ACKNOWLEDGEMENTS

Over the years in which I have pursued my interest in Thatcham's local history, many individuals have contributed in various ways to my knowledge and understanding of my adoptive home. Some have loaned – or given – me postcards and photographs; others have done the same with artifacts and written materials of different sorts; a few – some of these no longer with us – have shared with me treasured memories of their lives in old Thatcham before these were lost.

Whilst it would be impossible to mention all those who have helped me, I should like to record my gratitude to the following people whose contributions have made this publication possible: Mrs Rose Bellis, Mr Jeff Brooks, Mr Robert Brown, Mr David Canning, Mrs Aleithia Carnell, Mr Bert Chandler, Mr Ted Chandler, Mrs B. Child, Mr Birt Claridge, Mrs Denise Cochrane, Mr and Mrs David Cooper, Mr Geoff Davies, Mrs Janet Dowd, Mr John Eggleton, Mr Stan Eggleton, Mr Mike Evans, Mr Clifford Fuller, Mrs Dorothy Gardiner, Mrs Constance Gilbert, Mr John Giles, Mrs Jan Gray, Mr Harold Grinham, Mr Gordon Hands, Mr Bert Harfitt, Mr Hubert Hawkins, Mrs Janice Hawkins, Mr Graham Holbon, Mr John Holbon, Mrs Sue Hopson, Mr Bert Hunt, Mr Cecil Hunt, Mr John Hutchings, Mrs Kath Hutchings, Mr Ron Joyce, Mrs Beatrice Jones, Mr Maurice Lane, Mr Malcolm Langford, Miss Gwen Lawrence, Mrs Wendy Liversidge, Mr Ron Lovegrove, Miss Anne McAvey, Mrs Olive McJohnston, Mr Joe Mace, Revd Tom Moffatt, Mr Basil Parsons, Mr and Mrs Jim Rogers, Mrs Margery Roper, Mr Cyril Rutter, Mr Wilfred Rutter, Mr Fred Shadlock, Mr George Slade, Mrs Mary Smith, Mr Tony Stacey, Mr and Mrs William Stanbrook, Mr Graeme Stewart, Mr George Stocker, Mr Les Sugden, Mrs Jenny Thornton, Mr Laurie Turner, Mrs Hilda Warner, Mr David Wootton, Mr and Mrs Bruno Zornow.

Last – but by no means least – my wife Ann, who shared the work of compiling the available material into *The Book of Thatcham*.

St Mary's Church viewed from the south-west in the early-twentieth century, when there was still a pond (now filled in) at this corner of the churchyard.

Chapter I

Continuity and Change in the Community

A History of Thatcham House

Thatcham House is a building of some merit. It earned a mention in Nikolaus Pevsner's *Buildings of England*, where it is described as 'Victorian Gothic' and as possessing 'brick and stone dressings, with an eccentrically placed turret'. It was erected on land belonging to Mr Mount of Wasing. Once the site of an ancient village pound for straying animals, tradition has it that the land was used as a gypsy encampment from the mid-nineteenth century. Thatcham House was built for the Revd Hezekiah Martin – vicar of Thatcham from 1866 until 1889 – after he had married into the Tull family.

Hezekiah Martin – not a local man – was born in 1834. He attended Corpus Christi College in Cambridge and was awarded the degree of Master of Arts. He was ordained in 1858 and successively held curacies in Sussex, Stepney, Norfolk and Folkestone prior to his appointment to the vicarage of Thatcham in 1866. On arriving in the village, he took up residence at the Old Vicarage in Lower Way. Within months of coming to Thatcham, Revd Martin suffered a personal tragedy: already married, and the father of a young son named Basil, his wife died shortly after giving birth to another child.

By now Revd Martin had made the acquaintance of the Tull family, for they worshipped regularly at his church. 'Squire' Richard Tull died in 1868, bringing sadness upon his family as well. Soon, however, the families of Martin and Tull were united by the joy of a wedding. Banns of marriage between Hezekiah Martin and Isabel Sarah Tull were published in the Parish Church during March 1869. Miss Tull was the only daughter of the late Richard Tull – born in 1840, she was now a woman in her late twenties. Revd Martin and Miss Tull were married at Thatcham's Parish Church on 1 April 1869.

It was at this time that the building of Thatcham House was commissioned – situated off Station Road, it lay between the Parish Church and Crookham House. The house occupied its own grounds, being surrounded by gardens, including a kitchen garden/orchard and a sunken rose garden, with extensive lawns on its southern side. The perimeter of the property was well screened by the trees that were planted around the house.

Access to the house was by a gravel drive from Station Road to the northern side of the building where there was a turning-circle for coaches: the latter were kept in the stable-cum-coach-house in the north-eastern corner of the property. The house

Thatcham House in the early-twentieth century, viewed from the rear and showing the carriage drive which led past the house to the coach-house and stables.

contained over 30 rooms including a large drawing room, a dining room, an impressive entrance hall and several bedrooms. The drawing room led off into a conservatory where hot and humid conditions were maintained by the gardener to produce a variety of ferns, lilies, fuchsias and other plants. At the eastern end of the house were the servants' quarters.

An enigmatic feature of the house is the embattled tower. Its original use is obscure – it may simply have been a folly. It is very narrow inside (being about 10 feet wide). It has no built-in staircase and only a few very small windows. Perhaps it is no coincidence that it is some 60 feet high – almost the same height as the tower of the Parish Church (which is exactly 66 feet) – and has a bell on its outside wall. The roof may be reached by a trap door but as the retaining wall is rather low this is not the place for the nervous on a windy day. From the roof the Parish Church can be seen to the west and, interestingly, to the south Crookham House can be picked out among the trees.

Thatcham House was completed in about two years and Revd Martin and his new wife were in residence by the autumn of 1871, raising their family here. Mrs Martin produced 11 children in as many years. One child, Cecil Danvers, died an infant of six months of age – born on the 29 March 1874, he died on the 20 September of the same year and was buried in the churchyard with the first Mrs Martin. Isabel Martin herself died on 11 June 1881, soon after the birth of her eleventh child, perhaps worn out by childbirth. She too was buried in the Parish

Churchyard and her funeral took place before Albert Leslie, her last child, was christened – Revd Martin was a widower once more!

With 13 children to look after, it is not surprising to find that Revd Martin married for a third time, but within a few years his health began to fail. He became quite ill and was obliged to spend some time away from the village convalescing. At last, in January 1889, Revd Martin resigned as Thatcham's vicar. He and his family went to live at Clevedon in Somerset where he died on the 29 June 1889, at the age of 55 years.

Revd Martin's body was returned to Thatcham for burial in the family vault in the Parish Churchyard. The coffin was brought by train to the local railway station on 4 July, and then conveyed in a carriage to the churchyard. A *Newbury Weekly News* report describes how the funeral cortege '... moved slowly along the winding road, and past Thatcham House – Mr Martin's late residence which he built'. His third wife and six of his children from his previous marriages attended his funeral; his brother-in-law, 'Squire' Tull of Crookham, also came to pay his last respects.

Two years later Mrs Martin returned briefly to Thatcham, from Clevedon where the family now resided permanently. As a memorial to her late husband, she had paid for new chimes and a face to be fitted to the clock in the tower of the Parish Church. Designed by Stalwood of Reading and built by Benson of London, the new clock was officially handed over by Mrs Martin at a ceremony held on the afternoon of Saturday 22 August, 1891. High up on the church tower, the clock remains the official memorial to Revd Martin today; but down in Station Road there is another, more impressive, memorial to him – Thatcham House.

After the Martin family had moved out of Thatcham House in 1889, Mr John Hart Player took up residence there with his family. His daughters – the 'Misses Player' – were actively involved in the village musical events which were then staged regularly in Thatcham. The Player family vacated the house in May of 1893, whereupon it became the home of Mr Richard Samuel Chattock for the next nine years.

The new century saw a celebrated military family take up residence. Thatcham House became the home of the Turner family in 1902: Major Charles Turner was born in 1862, the eldest son of Robert Turner of Bishopsfield in Nottinghamshire. Between 1881 and 1902, he had served with the Royal Berkshire Regiment and came to Thatcham on retiring from the army. Here, however, be continued in public service, being elected a District Councillor for Thatcham in 1907 and serving as a JP for Berkshire and as Deputy Lieutenant for the county.

Major Turner had been twice married – his first wife, Ella, daughter of Charles James Thornton, had died in 1887. His second wife, Jane Elizabeth, was a member of the famous Redvers Buller family, one of whom had won the VC in the Zululand Campaign of 1879 and then earned a national reputation as a General in the Boer War. Major Turner had five children by his second wife, four sons and a daughter, and all of them came to live at Thatcham House.

The Turners' sons also served in the forces and – given their mother's background – it is not surprising perhaps that they too distinguished themselves. The eldest son, born in 1893, was Alexander Buller Turner. He became a Second Lieutenant and served with the 1st Battalion of the Royal Berkshire Regiment. When the First World War broke out in 1914, A.B. Turner went with his regiment to fight on the Western Front.

On 28 September 1915, he made a daring attack on enemy positions at 'Slag Alley', Fosse, near Vermelles in France – throwing bombs incessantly, he drove the Germans back 150 yards, allowing British reserves to advance with very little loss. For this action he won the VC but he was wounded in the attack and died on 1 October 1915, aged only 22. A.B. Turner was buried in the military cemetery at Chocque, France, but a

A 1905 close-up view of Thatcham House, built about 1870 for the Revd Hezekiah Martin. This imposing Victorian Gothic house became home to the Turner family in 1902.

A postcard view of 1915 showing Thatcham House from the south – it was at about this time that the Turner family, then in residence, received the sad news of the death of their son Alexander in the First World War.

wall tablet to his memory was placed in the Parish Church in Thatcham.

In 1918, the War Office Trophies Committee offered Thatcham a German Howitzer field gun and carriage that had been captured during the conflict by A.B. Turner's Battalion. A special Parish Council meeting was held on 26 May 1919, at which the offer was discussed. There was some dissent but the offer was eventually accepted and the German gun duly arrived in Thatcham where it was restored and painted.

At that same Parish Council meeting the possibility of creating a memorial to the other 100 men of the village who had laid down their lives in the war was discussed, although precise details were not finalised until later. In the event, a memorial, designed by Sir Charles Nicholson of London and built by an Oxford firm, was erected at the stop of the Broadway green (it was moved to the Bath Road in 1966).

The memorial and gun were formally dedicated at a ceremony held on Armistice Day, Thursday 11 November 1920. Both had been draped with large Union flags for the ceremony. General E.T. Dickson of the Royal Berkshire Regiment unveiled the war memorial and Major and Mrs Turner of Thatcham House unveiled the German gun. (The gun was disposed of as scrap in 1940.)

Between the wars, life at Thatcham House went on much as before. However, there were now fewer servants and the coach had given way to a car for which a chauffeur was occasionally hired. There are still people in Thatcham today who remember the Turner family well and some were actually employed at the house. By this time the servants included a housemaid, parlour-maid, between-maid, butler, cook, nanny and two gardeners; the bell on the tower was rung to call the gardeners in for meals. The three maids and the nanny lived-in as their working day began very early indeed.

For the family, life was more leisurely. In his younger days, Major Turner had been on hunting expeditions the trophies he had brought back with him now decorated the entrance hall of the house, with its polished oak floor and ornate iron banister. On the floor and walls were the skins and heads of buffaloes, rhinos, lions and tigers. Now Major Turner worked quietly in his study, enjoying his retirement.

He died on 20 May 1926, and was buried in Thatcham cemetery. His wife and children stayed on at the house. The youngest son, Mark, was given cricket coaching on the lawn. The house also possessed a tennis court and a squash court (next to the coach-house). The daughter, 'Miss Turner' (she was still unmarried) became the local Guide Captain and the girls often met at Thatcham House.

The other two sons – Victor and Cecil – were in the Army and Navy respectively, and when the Second World War broke out in 1939 both served with distinction. Victor Buller Turner, born in 1900, had

The unveiling of Thatcham's War Memorial on Armistice Day, November 1920 – General Dickson (Royal Berks Regt) steps forward to unveil the memorial as Major Turner unveils the German gun.

been commissioned in 1918 and became a Lieutenant Colonel serving with the 2nd Battalion of the Rifle Brigade.

V.B. Turner served in the Western Desert of Egypt. On 27 October 1942, he led his battalion 4,000 yards across difficult terrain – under cover of darkness – to capture an enemy position. His men took 40 prisoners and held the position for the rest of the day; repeated German attacks were repulsed and 35 enemy tanks destroyed. V.B. Turner was awarded the VC for this action, and although wounded he survived the war.

Back in England in 1942, the news of Victor's award – coupled with that of his late brother, Alexander – made the Turner family nationally newsworthy. The *Daily Express* reported:

A greetings telegram arriving at the back door of a tall red house in the village of Thatcham, near Newbury, tonight said that Victor Buller Turner had won the VC. To Mrs Charles Buller Turner it meant that she was the mother of two VC winners.

The report went on to say that Mrs Turner was looking forward to the day when Victor would be decorated by the King: her pride may well have been tinged with sadness, however, for hanging in frames above the fireplace at Thatcham House were Alexander's VC and the letter from an earlier monarch conveying 'sincere regret' that his death deprived him of the same honour.

The Turner family's connection with Thatcham was severed shortly after the Second World War ended in 1945. V.B. Turner returned to the village but his mother, Mrs Jane Turner, died on 9 July 1946, and was buried with her husband in Thatcham cemetery. About two years later, Thatcham House was vacated by the remaining members of the family and put up for sale.

The Turners' grown-up children moved to Bungay, on the Norfolk-Suffolk border, and rented a house on Brigadier Bill Carr's Ditchingham estate. Victor Turner died there in August 1972, aged 72 – his VC was posthumously presented to the Rifle Brigade Museum, Winchester. (Elder brother Alexander's VC was posthumously presented to the Royal Berkshire Regiment.) The sister – real name Jane, like her mother, but always known as 'Miss Turner' (she never married) or 'Millie' – lived out her remaining years in a cottage in the nearby village of Hedenham, Norfolk. She died in September 1996, at the ripe old age of 101.

Meanwhile, the family's old residence back in Thatcham proved too big for modern family requirements and remained unoccupied for some years after 1948. The final phase in the life of Thatcham House as residential accommodation was not unlike that of many other large old houses in the postwar period.

In 1951 it was 'modernised' and converted into three self-contained flatlets. Doors were bricked up, passages blocked off and the spacious entrance hall divided by partition walls. In the days when Major Charles Turner lived at the house, the entrance hall was decorated with tigers' heads and other trophies, brought back from hunting expeditions he had been on as a young man, but those days were now long gone.

A view across what was then a lawned garden to the front of Thatcham House in about 1920 – this area has now been built on and is occupied by Turner's Drive.

Within a few years, Mr Bruno Zornow, a local builder, who lived in the house for a time, had acquired the house and grounds. Later, Mr Zornow built himself a modern detached house on the northern edge of the grounds and continued to let Thatcham House as flatlets.

Then, during the early 1960s, Mr Zornow built more detached houses across the lawns on the south side of the grounds. This development was named 'Turner's Drive' in 1964 in memory of the distinguished family who had once lived in the main house. The original carriage entrance leading off Station Road was blocked when more modern houses were erected and the coach-house/stable it

led to was used by Mr Zornow to store the double glazing he imported as part of his work as a builder.

On the eastern side of the old house, the 35 fruit trees in the kitchen garden were replaced by a block of flats named 'Orchard Court', whilst on the western side the 300 bushes in the sunken rose garden gave way to another block of flats named 'Rosen Court' (the German plural for 'rose', as Mr Zornow was himself of German nationality). In the period when American servicemen based at Greenham Common occupied many of the flats, this part of Thatcham was nicknamed 'Little America'!

By the 1970s, Thatcham House was over a century old and beginning to show signs of wear and tear. It eventually deteriorated so much that the three flatlets were vacated. Newbury District Council finally issued a closing order on the house in 1980 and Mr Zornow was faced with a massive bill for renovation – up to £20,000 for roof repairs alone, for example.

He decided that it would be uneconomic to restore the house as residential accommodation and proposed instead to convert the building into office space. Although controversial in some ways, this plan did ensure the continued existence of one of Thatcham's grandest old houses and was duly effected. By 1988, the main house, along with the old coach-house, had been converted into some 25 offices.

Sadly, Bruno Zornow died on 31 May 1990, but the house is still owned by his family in the form of the Barbara Zornow Settlement Trust. Internally, Thatcham House is now home to hi-tech businesses, currently being leased to computer companies and similar organisations. Externally, although now hemmed in on all sides by modern development, it is still possible to stand in front of the house and imagine – from here, in times past, the families of Martin and Turner made their contributions to the shaping of local – and national – history.

Today, these people are already half-forgotten and memory of them is rapidly receding but if you 'seek their monument' just stand and look – at Thatcham House!

The Changing Heart of Thatcham

The Broadway (or Broad Street, as it was once known) is the historic heart of 'Old Thatcham'. It was the market place of the medieval borough and the hub of the old village, around which the life of Thatcham revolved – it is not surprising that there are the remains of an old market cross in the Broadway today! During the coaching era, 40 coaches a day called here, either at the King's Head or the White Hart. By the nineteenth century, there was a maypole in the Broadway and it has been the venue for numerous events in Thatcham's past – such as coronation celebrations – when it rang with the sound of anvil firing.

Above: The Broadway, Thatcham, c.1913, looking south. Mr Charles George Brown's motor works is on the left.

Left: The Broadway green has been the venue for village celebrations for centuries – in this case probably for the coronation of King Edward VII in August 1902.

Right: An early colour postcard showing the view looking north into the Broadway from the top of Station Road. The building on the left served as the old Parish Workhouse until 1837 and was demolished in 1959.

In late-Victorian times, the character of the Broadway was more residential than today. There were then no fewer than six families of Pinnock living in the Broadway (and one more around the corner in the High Street): this must have caused the village postman Harry Wise, a few headaches! One of these families was that of Edmund Pinnock, who kept a coal yard on the east side of the Broadway. He was appointed official carrier to the GWR in 1869 and thereafter his wagonette plied to and from the railway station. (The yard has disappeared under a shopping development today).

At the bottom of the Broadway was a house called Montana: here lived William Draper, Thatcham's registrar-cum-relieving officer from 1872 until 1920. On Friday mornings, in all types of weather, the old and poor of the parish queued outside the house for their weekly dole of 1s. and perhaps an order for bread. Today, the house is still there but thankfully the sad queues have long gone.

On a happier note, there used to be an annual circus on the Broadway green. Having pitched its tent, the company would put on the usual turns – the clowns went down well with the village children! One year, the *Newbury Weekly News* reported the arrival of the circus, which put on three performances on Thursday, Friday and Saturday evenings, '... a considerable number of the inhabitants being present to witness the equestrian and other amusements provided'. One old Thatcham resident remembered other such circuses at which there was a pony able to discover which boy in the audience was 'guilty of stealing his mother's sugar'.

At the end of the nineteenth century, Thatcham's Broadway had changed very little compared with its mediaeval state. The turn of the century, however, was to witness an increasingly rapid rate of change that would alter its character drastically – and almost certainly not for the better. Nevertheless, there was one last flourish from 'Old Thatcham' when one of the village's distinguished personages paid for the first seats to be built around the stump of the ancient market cross.

The seats were erected at the expense of Samuel Barfield in 1892. He was the son of John Barfield of the 'Priory' in Church Lane and later had a two-volume history of Thatcham published. 'A hearty vote of thanks' was proposed to Mr Barfield at a parish vestry meeting, for his kindness and 'the general interest he has always taken in the village of Thatcham'. The vestry minutes record that Barfield intended his seats to be for the use of 'aged persons of Thatcham' – one wonders what he would think if he knew how his seats would be (ab)used by future generations?

To mark the turn of the century, Miss A.L. Henry of Colthrop had an oak tree planted in the Broadway next to the market cross – it has witnessed 100 years of change in the historic heart of Thatcham. The death of Queen Victoria in 1901 and the accession of King Edward VII marked the beginning of a new age as well as a new century.

The pace of life in Thatcham began to quicken, although it would not be until the second half of the twentieth century that major changes occurred. The Broadway was still surrounded by ancient timber-

Above left: *The view into Churchgate from the bottom of the Broadway c.1960 – a view that has changed little since this date.*

Above right: *An early colour postcard showing the bottom of the Broadway, looking into Churchgate, in about 1905 – it would be foolhardy to stand in the middle of the road like this today!*

Left: *The view into Churchgate from the bottom of the Broadway in the 1970s – only the growth of road traffic has changed the scene.*

The Broadway looking north in about 1900: in the background the tall chimney of Stephen Parr's axle-tree foundry can be seen on the skyline.

The view past existing premises at the top of the Broadway into one of the old alleyways, which led off the main street here – note the ancient house, architecturally interesting but now demolished (extreme right).

The occasion of the official handing over to the villagers of Thatcham of the Tomlin fountain in July 1911 – it was built at the expense of Mrs Ann Tomlin, an old resident of the village.

framed buildings, although their façades were modified as they ceased to be family homes and were given over instead to commercial uses.

The business life of the Broadway was also changing. Behind the shops at the top of the Broadway there had been an 'axle-tree' foundry – its tall chimney had been a landmark for miles around. With the decline of horse-drawn vehicles, such a trade could not last: Stephen Parr was the last man to follow the calling here but he gave up in 1904 and the tall chimney of his foundry was later demolished.

On the other hand, the age of the motorcar was just dawning. C.G. Brown began trading as a cycle repairer in premises next door to Parr's. As a sign of progress, he erected a public clock outside his shop, illuminated by electricity from his own private supply. When his sons began to undertake motor repairs from a new garage alongside the King's Head in September 1911, the clock was re-erected there. (This family firm ceased trading in 1990).

At the northern end, the old 'Thatcham Slums' began to disappear: the 'slums' were a mass of alleyways – including 'Clinker Alley' and 'Soapsuds

Alley' – extending behind the High Street shops, most of which were demolished in about 1911. In the summer of that same year, the road surface in the Broadway was first tarred and metalled.

It was a busy year in other ways: in July, the Thatcham fountain was handed over to the people of Thatcham by its donor, Mrs Ann Tomlin of Sydney Lodge in Station Road. Built over a 140-feet-deep well, the fountain provided drinking water for man and beast by means of a fountain housed in an attractive shelter with a horse trough on its northern side.

War intervened, bringing changes of its own. Afterwards, a war memorial dedicated to the men of Thatcham who gave their lives in the First World War – was erected in the Broadway in 1920. Unveiled on Armistice Day that year, it stood at the top of the green until moved to its present site on the Bath Road in 1966. Near to the memorial when it stood in the Broadway was placed the German gun (a Howitzer, captured by the Royal Berkshire Regiment during the war). Newly restored and painted, it was intended as a memorial to the Thatcham VC winner, A.B. Turner.

Just prior to the outbreak of the Second World War,

An aerial view looking north to Thatcham Broadway in 1953, when the woodturnery works of John Brown & Sons (foreground) was still operational – it closed in 1958.

public conveniences were built behind the Tomlin fountain, which itself became merely a shelter, no longer providing water. The German gun was disposed of as scrap in 1940, when a new war had broken out. At about that time, an air-raid shelter was built on the green. (It was not demolished until 1960.)

At the bottom of the Broadway, the long-established woodturnery – which also had its factory chimney – was eventually demolished too. The woodturning trade was once the village's major source of employment and this site had originally been operated by Messrs Pinnock. Records show that Stephen Pinnock senr was a 'mopstick maker' here as early as 1815. Messrs Brown took over the factory in 1889 – the founder, John Brown, had started his own mopstick factory in Thatcham in 1847.

During the twentieth century, Messrs Brown came to dominate the woodturning trade in Thatcham and concentrated their production at the factory at the bottom of the Broadway. At their centenary in 1947 the firm treated its 70 employees to a celebration dinner but it remained in business for only a few years more and finally closed down in 1958. (The

premises were eventually demolished and a residential development – named Nideggen Close – built on the site in 1987).

Elsewhere in the Broadway, things were changing too. At premises on its western side, Frederick Spanswick – who came to Thatcham in 1915 – had established a motor coach business, running the first motor bus in the district. Thatcham's Co-operative supermarket (originally situated at the corner of Bath

Thatcham Broadway looking north in the 1950s when the war memorial was still on the green: note the double-decker bus at the stop on the left.

Road and Green Lane) moved to this site in the 1960s. (It was then extended after the old Infant School next door was demolished in 1979.)

More modern shopping developments came to the Broadway. On the eastern side, the old workhouse was demolished and replaced by a parade of shops named Tanner House and officially opened by TV personality John Slater (of *Z Cars* fame) in 1960. Not far away, a new VG supermarket was built in 1969 and also opened by a TV personality, Ted Ray.

The pre-war fountain and toilet were demolished in 1969 and new public conveniences were erected the following year. The 1970 toilet block was built to a design with which a Newbury man won a competition but the people of Thatcham never liked it. No one was sorry when it was demolished on 24 October 1996, and a modem structure erected in its place. The new conveniences – including baby changing and disabled facilities – were built at a cost of £133,000 and officially opened on the morning of Wednesday 7 May 1997, by Mr John Morgan (Chairman of Newbury District Council).

The largest development in the Broadway is the Kingsland Centre, built at a cost of £5.8 million and opened in 1986. The first shop to open there in September 1986, was a Gateway supermarket – it became Somerfields with effect from November 1991, when local ex-GP Dr Deborah Bradley-Moore arrived in a vintage Rolls-Royce to cut a ribbon at a special ceremony. (It became Waitrose in 2000).

The view into the Broadway looking south from Chapel Street in about 1970, with the (then) new toilet block (since replaced).

Looking north out of the Broadway, c.1980, over the base of the old market cross. Even this view has changed now, with the addition of traffic lights, pedestrianisation and the Millennium Monument.

The view north along the western side of the Broadway green in 1976 – various changes have since taken place, including the disappearance of the cottages (left) for the Co-op supermarket extension.

Looking into Pinnock's Yard on the eastern side of the Broadway in about 1985 – the business relocated to Piper's Lane prior to the building of the Kingsland Centre here a few years later.

Looking north out of the Broadway into Chapel Street in about 1985, prior to pedestrianisation of parts of the road layout here and the erection of the Millennium Monument in 2000.

The Broadway Courtyard development opened in 1987: the first business to locate there – a hairdresser's – was opened by TV personality Michaela Strachan, although the courtyard as a whole was not officially opened until May 1988, by disc jockey 'Diddy' David Hamilton.

Around the green itself, the roads have been subject to a number of changes over the years including a variety of different traffic flows and parking arrangements. Then, under the terms of a 'town centre improvement scheme', the most recent works were completed in October 1996. They involved resurfacing the green and the introduction of partial pedestrianisation. However, nothing that happens in the Broadway can alter the fact that this always has been, and always will be, the historic heart of Thatcham.

St Mary's Church and graveyard seen from the south-west in about 1914 – the time when Mr A.R. Tull was buried in the family tomb (seen at the foot of the tower).

Funeral of a Country Gentleman

A Parish Church is a mute witness to many an historic occasion. In the case of Thatcham's Parish Church, amongst the most notable such events are the funerals of local dignitaries, including those of the squires of the old village. Take, for example, the funeral of Mr Albert Richard Tull. He was described in a contemporary *Newbury Weekly News* report as a 'Berkshire Notability' and his funeral brought a large and distinguished assemblage of mourners to St Mary's churchyard nearly a century ago.

Mr Tull was the squire of Crookham and, effectively, of Thatcham too (in the absence of a resident

The Tull family residence – Crookham House, viewed from the south-west, as it was in the early years of the twentieth century.

Crookham House (west elevation). Built in the mid-nineteenth century as the residence of the Tull family, the house still stands but is now divided into apartments.

The interior of the Parish Church as it was around the time of Mr Tull's funeral – there are various memorial plaques to members of the Tull family on the walls of the nave.

squire in the latter place). His grandfather had begun the family link with Crookham in the late-eighteenth century. The estate subsequently passed to his father, Richard Tull, who – with his wife Sarah – lived at Crookham House. It was here that Albert Richard was born on 8 October 1835. He was educated at Exeter College, Oxford, and succeeded to the estate upon his father's death in 1868.

In 1873, A.R. Tull married Miss Florence Blyth, daughter of Mr James Blyth of Woolhampton House. Following their honeymoon, on return to Thatcham, their carriage from the railway station to Crookham House was escorted by members of the Royal Berkshire Yeomanry Cavalry, in which Mr Tull then held the rank of Captain. The couple had four daughters and one son, whose birth – as heir to the estate – was marked by hospitable entertainment at Crookham House.

A typical country gentleman, A.R. Tull served in many an official capacity. He was a JP from 1867 and High Sheriff of Berkshire in 1875. From 1876, for 29 years, he chaired the Newbury Divisional Petty Sessions and, later, the Berkshire Quarter Sessions. He became a founder member of Berkshire County Council (founded in 1889), and eventually its Chairman.

Locally, Mr Tull also served on Thatcham's Parish Council (formed in 1895), including a spell as Chairman. He was a keen politician and (as might be expected) a staunch Conservative. He chaired the South Berkshire Conservative Association and was vice-president of the Newbury Conservative Club. Mr Tull was a trustee of the Thatcham and Midgham Friendly Society and subscribed to its funds. He

The approach to St Mary's Church from Station Road and the Broadway in around 1914 – the route of the cortège on the day of 'Squire' Tull's funeral.

worshipped regularly at Thatcham's Parish Church, and frequently read the lessons.

He seems to have had a special interest in education. He was a trustee of Thatcham's Bluecoat School and paid for the rebuilding of the old Broadway Infant School in 1875. For many years he allowed a barn at St George's Farm, on the Crookham estate, to be used as the venue for the annual treat for the school children of the village. Apart from his public activities, he did much for individual parishioners and families living in Thatcham.

Sadly, Mr Tull's health started to deteriorate in the early years of the twentieth century. His death occurred on 13 November 1914, and he was buried in

The funeral procession of 'Squire' Tull of Crookham House arriving at St Mary's Church in November 1914 – the choir boys are leading the cortège.

The funeral cortège arriving at St Mary's Church – Mr Tull's coffin is preceded by Revd Edward Chamberlain. Mr A.S.B. Tull (son and heir) is following.

'Squire' Tull is laid to rest in the family grave – seen from the tower, a large assemblage of mourners pay their respects.

a family vault in St Mary's churchyard four days later. The funeral of such a distinguished person was well attended:

High and low, rich and poor, gathered in large numbers from the county and the countryside to pay their last tribute to one whom they had loved as a friend, respected as a counsellor, looked up to as a master.

The clergy and choir met the cortège at the church gates. As well as Thatcham's vicar (Revd Edward Chamberlain), the Venerable Archdeacon of Berkshire (Canon Ducat) and the Rural Dean (Revd A.W. Edwards) officiated. A detachment of the Berkshire Constabulary, under Supt Gamble, lined the pathway. A company of National Reservists from Newbury Racecourse Detention Camp, under Major Langford formed a guard of honour.

The workmen from the Crookham estate (where all non-essential work stopped for the day) lined up outside the church and fell in behind the procession. Children from the Crookham School, with their master, Mr J.S. Cole, waited in the churchyard. A muffled peal was rung before the service, and a half-muffled peal afterwards, as the body was laid to rest in a vault where A.R. Tull's father and wife (who died in 1898) were also buried.

Numerous family members and friends were present. Other mourners ranged from county councillors and magistrates to local villagers and humble cottagers. Among them were the Member of Parliament, Mr William Mount; the Lord Lieutenant of Berkshire, Mr J.H. Benyon; the Chairman of Newbury Division of County Magistrates, Mr E.E. Martin-Atkins; the Chief Constable of Berkshire, Major Poulton; the Chairman of Berkshire County Council, Dr Robert Mowbray, and of Thatcham Parish Council, Mr Arthur Brown.

There can have been few occasions when so many VIPs joined with the inhabitants of Thatcham at a funeral in the Parish Churchyard. For all the sadness of the event, it was a beautifully fine and peaceful autumnal day. The family vault was to be opened once more, 40 years later, when Mr Tull's son and heir (A.S.B. Tull, who died in 1954) was buried. This was the last burial in the Tull tomb, and for that matter in the Parish Churchyard.

The Tull tomb in St Mary's churchyard as it is today – the last interment in the family grave was that of Mr A.S.B. Tull in 1954.

Chapter II

Helping People, People Helping

Keeping up the Good Work

Today, the very notion of 'charity' may seem to be something of an anachronism – living in a modern society with welfare state provision, it is difficult to appreciate that charity once made the difference between a hard life and a comfortable one or perhaps even between life and death! However, at the beginning of the twentieth century, the subject of charity was topical and controversial, at both national level and here in the old village of Thatcham.

On Tuesday 19 June 1906, 15 local worthies sat down to a meeting with representatives of the Charity Commission, who had travelled to Thatcham

Chapel Street looking west from outside the New Inn at the end of the nineteenth century – next to the inn is Loundyes' Almshouse as it appeared at this date.

These cottages in Chapel Street were known as the Nine-shilling Houses – seen in about 1900 the row comprised four part-thatched, part-tiled charity cottages. The single cottage (left) was demolished in 1904 to make way for the village's new police station.

from London. The meeting was to be an 'inquiry' into the charities of the 'ancient parish of Thatcham'; the venue (21 Bath Road) was the office of Mr G.J. Fyfield, clerk to the trustees of the parochial charities. Those present with him included the Revd David Pierce (vicar of Thatcham), A. Brown (overseer), B. Mecey (Parish Council clerk) and Mrs Hunt (descendant of the founder of an early charity).

Thatcham's charities dated back to the early-fifteenth century. They had been established on an *ad hoc* basis by benefactors with varied motives and with endowments large and small, depending on their means. In their wills, some had left land and other property to raise rental income; others monies to provide a regular income from investments. After the decease of the benefactors, the management of these charities was initially left in the hands of trustees, but with the passage of time the vicar and churchwardens often assumed this responsibility.

By this date, most of the documents relating to the foundation of the parochial charities had long since been lost but those assembled at this inquiry had access to two vital sources – the reports of three earlier Charity Commission inquiries in Thatcham, for 1819, 1837 and 1899. The first had dealt specifically with a local charity school (of which more later); the last had been instigated by Thatcham's newly formed Parish Council in 1895, when it applied to the Charity Commissioners claiming a voice in the management of some of the village's charities.

At the beginning of the twentieth century, some of Thatcham's charities were 500 years old (and many had been mismanaged over the years, either by design or by neglect). The oldest parochial charities dated from 1413 and together made up the 'Church Estate', comprising a dozen or so endowments of land and property, income from which was intended as a 'church rate' for church repairs. By 1906, however, other charities had been 'appropriated by the vicar and churchwardens', who managed them all, even when this was not the benefactors' intention.

The range of charities was considerable. Thomas Loundyes' Charity (of 1445) had established an almshouse in Chapel Street where poor travellers might be temporarily accommodated along with more permanent poor persons of the parish. By 1906 the property was home to six almswomen (no men had ever been known to be appointed); each received about 4s. (20p) cash and a hundredweight of coal weekly, along with £10 or more of firewood per annum. At the end of 1905 this charity's gross income from rents on its endowed properties was some £73p.a.

Another significant local charity was John Hunt's (of 1590), whose original deed had been lost but there was a parchment copy in the church chest. He had effectively set up two endowments, one for his 'poor kinsfolk' and another for the parish poor generally. This resulted in the building of several cottages in Thatcham Broadway. Richard Hunt occupied the poor kinsman's house in 1906; three widows occupied the others, each receiving 1s. (5p) a week and 5 cwt of coal at Christmas. At the end of 1905 this charity's total gross income was about £28p.a.

Thatcham's other parochial charities at this date were varied. Two – Richard Bye's (1585) and John Winchcombe's (1605) – had been combined following a recommendation in the 1837 Charity Commissioners' report. They noted that in the previous year the churchwardens had doled out the annual income from Winchcombe's benefaction in the form of sixpences – to no fewer than 1,080 men, women and children in Thatcham (some 40 per cent of the population of the village as it then was). This was judged 'more hurtful than beneficial' and discouraged for future distributions.

In 1906, the net income from Bye's and Winchcombe's charities was distributed half in coal and the rest in money only to the deserving poor of the parish. In that same year, John Heardman's Gift (1594) produced an annual Easter 'dole' of £6 between four poor parishioners; Thomas Goddard's Bequest (1680) produced an annual Christmas payment of 2s. (10p) each for nominated parish paupers; and William Northway's Bequest (1820) saw an annual distribution of bread on St Thomas's Day plus annual cash payments to Thatcham's three 'oldest poor single men'.

There were even smaller charities. John Sargood (1826) invested £100 in Navy stocks, the interest to be divided annually between the six poor widows in Loundyes' Almshouse. Elizabeth Coxe Bailey (sister of Francis) – who died in 1859 – left an investment of £450 in her will, the interest therefrom to be divided between 12 each of the parish's poorest men and women. Local historian Samuel Barfield – who died in 1899 – left a legacy of £2,000, the income from which was distributed by the vicars of Thatcham and Cold Ash in the form of cash, coal and clothing.

At the end of the meeting in 1906, Thatcham's worthies and the Charity Commissioners adopted the 1899 scheme and cleared up many irregularities in the parochial charities. However, the whole thing remained piecemeal; indeed, it was added to in later years by a few more small charities, one of which was created by George James Fyfield himself. Upon his death in 1943, he left a legacy in his will and his office at 21 Bath Road (where the 1906 meeting had been held) as a reading room. He also left his library of music and historical books to Thatcham's parish charity trustees.

A decade later, the patchwork nature of Thatcham's

charities was making things difficult for the trustees. The Ministry of Health required improvement works on Loundyes' Almshouse in Chapel Street, the cost of which could not be met under the existing scheme. Limited resources reduced the number of 'gift tickets' which were still distributed each Christmas. Accordingly, a new scheme for the village charities was effected (and confirmed in 1958) whereby the existing charities were grouped together as either 'General Poor Charities' or 'Almshouse Charities'.

The recent history of Thatcham's Parochial Charities has been one of further reorganisation for administrative purposes. Under a 1978 scheme the general poor charities became the 'Relief in Need Charity', offering similar help to the needy as statutory services (grants, loans and emergency benefits for special needs). Under a 1988 scheme the Almshouse Charity focused on accommodation for the elderly and the Charity Commissioners granted permission for new almshouses to be built here provided they were paid for 'out of the income and property' of John Hunt's Charity.

On the 400th anniversary of the establishment of this charity, new John Hunt Almshouses were ceremonially opened next to the existing Thomas Loundyes' Almshouses in Chapel Street. Built at a cost of £200,000 they were designed by Sutton & Griffin and erected by C.F. Allen, comprising four units (like Loundyes'). The official opening was performed by Mr Ron Higgins, Thatcham's deputy Mayor, on the evening of 25 July 1990. Mr David Wootton, chairman of the Almshouse Charity, said that it had taken 10 years to make the John Hunt Almshouses into 'a reality'.

In addition to the almshouses in Chapel Street, another almshouse with 6 units was built at the 'Dip', an old gravel pit at the junction of Lower Way and Green Lane. The land was purchased from the Church of England's Oxford Diocesan Board by Trencherwood plc, who erected several houses here – including the new almshouse, built at a cost of £310,000. Named the 'Nine-shilling House' – after an earlier charity – it was handed over by Trencherwood chief executive Mr John Norgate to the charity chairman Mr David Wootton at a ceremony held on 20 April 1995.

In Sickness and in Health

In the days before the National Health Service was created, medical treatment was at a premium throughout the country. In Thatcham in the nineteenth century, the parish authorities secured the services of doctors to minister to the needs of the villagers' health. From about 1880, the health of the villagers became the responsibility of two Irish doctors, the brothers Lyon.

Dr Francis Henry Lyon had his practice at Sydney

The combined almshouse of Loundyes' and Hunt's Charities as they can be seen today fronting onto Chapel Street.

The Nine-shilling Houses in Chapel Street in 1931, with transportation of the period parked outside!

The four cottages for the parish poor belonging to John Hunt's Charity – located on the eastern side of Thatcham Broadway, they were demolished in 1979.

The official opening ceremony of the new John Hunt Almshouse adjacent to Loundyes' Almshouse in Chapel Street on 25 July 1990, with Ron Higgins (Thatcham deputy Mayor).

The handing over of the new Nine-shilling Houses at the 'Dip' on 20 April 1995 by John Norgate (Trencherwood chief executive) to David Wootton (Thatcham Parochial Charities chairman).

The new Nine-shilling Houses built in the 'Dip' to replace the earlier ones that stood in Chapel Street – they were completed in 1995.

The view along Chapel Street, looking east in about 1910 – the one time Queen's Head Inn is where Dr Lyons had his surgery in the nineteenth century.

Lodge in Station Road, where he dealt with the 'better class' of clientele. Richard Hawtrey Lyon – 'physician and surgeon' – had his surgery at 100 Chapel Street (the old village post office) and he cared for the less well-off in Thatcham – if they could get past his ferocious bulldog!

Around the same time, there was a hospital at Cold Ash although its patients seem not to have been locals. The Cold Ash Children's Hospital was established in 1886 through the generosity of Miss Agnes Bowditch. It was originally founded as a convalescent home in her private residence, but the house eventually became the nurses' home and a new hospital was built in the grounds.

By 1891 Miss Bowditch was the hospital's 'lady superintendent' – she had 12 members of staff who then cared for 17 patients, most of whom were from London and were suffering from respiratory illnesses. Their ages ranged from 3–15 years and there was a school at the hospital to cater for their educational needs.

It was felt that the bracing air and surrounding greenery at Cold Ash would benefit the patients, although the latter sometimes presented risks of its own. In about 1906 Revd Walter Grindle, Cold Ash's vicar (1873–1928), reported that a child has been bitten by an adder in overgrown furze by the roadside!

Cold Ash Children's Hospital closed in 1964; its last matron was Miss Annette Le Page and the last head teacher was Miss Ethel Sibley. (The building was demolished in about 1970 and the site is now occupied by Sewell Close, a small housing development named after Mr 'Lew' Sewell, who had been a fund-raiser for the hospital in his lifetime – he died in 1966).

Meanwhile, down in Thatcham, new doctors ministered to the health of the villagers. From about 1900 Dr T. Martin had assumed this responsibility; by the date of the First World War he had taken up residence at The Poplars on the Bath Road, which became the village surgery. Then owned by the Brown family, this property was also occupied at different times by Thatcham's later doctors (P. Ransom, J. Beagley and D. Bradley-Moore).

The latter doctor was in general practice here for three decades and became a much-loved local figure. She joined the practice at Thatcham after the Second World War and worked here until 1977. (She stayed on at The Poplars in retirement and died on 1 December, 1996.)

To support the work of the village doctors, a Thatcham Nursing Society had been founded early in 1900. A nurse was appointed at a fixed salary of £80p.a., raised by donations and subscriptions from local residents. Nurse Whitehouse held the post first: at the end of the first year, she had attended 26 patients altogether – 20 in Thatcham, four at Crookham, one at Cold Ash and one at Bucklebury – making 813 visits in their sickness and 426 in convalescence. After 19 years, Nurse Whitehouse retired, being succeeded briefly by Nurse Turner.

She was followed by Nurse Slade, who took up the post in 1921 and held it for many years – due to retire in 1954 'after 33 years' service', she was persuaded to stay on even longer! It was during Nurse Slade's time that a house was provided for the local nurse, in memory of Mrs Bramwell-Davis (who had been born Evelyn Mary Tull of Crookham House in 1880, and married Captain Percy Bramwell-Davis in 1905).

Mrs Bramwell-Davis was a county councillor and

Cold Ash Children's Hospital seen here in about 1903 – opened in 1892 as a cottage hospital, its patients were all children and one can be seen (centre) on crutches.

The Cold Ash Children's Hospital, showing the wards where children convalesced – many had respiratory illnesses and the fresh air at Cold Ash was thought to be beneficial.

Cold Ash, looking down the hill into Thatcham, c.1920.   The Post Office (left) was then kept by the Pocock family.

Cold Ash Children's Hospital, c.1930.   It was opened as a cottage hospital in 1892 and closed in 1964.

did much voluntary work herself, earning the OBE for her efforts. Work began on the nurse's house after she died in 1938 and was completed in November, 1939.

A plaque set in its wall records that: 'This house for the District Nurse was erected by public subscription in 1939 as a memorial to Mrs Bramwell-Davis, OBE in recognition of her valuable work for her country'.

When the National Health Service was set up in the postwar years, the nurse's house found new uses. The Thatcham branch of Age Concern was founded in July 1964, aiming to promote the well-being of the senior citizens of Thatcham and district. In 1984, the charity occupied Friendship House, Church Gate, which stands in the shadow of St Mary's Church. The house became a 'drop-in centre' for Thatcham Age Concern. (It has become a private house today).

As Thatcham grew into a town, new medical facilities were needed. In the one-time garden of The Poplars, a new Health Centre was built for Berkshire County Council by Arthur J. Chivers – it cost £324,842 to build and equip. It came fully into use in September, 1978 – 7 doctors, 7 nurses, 4 health visitors and 20 receptionists, secretaries and ancillaries then catered for 16,000 patients – a far cry indeed from Thatcham's old village medical provision!

The nurse's house in Churchgate – it was built for the Thatcham Nursing Society in 1939 but today has become a private residence.

The Poplars on the Bath Road at Thatcham – this was the village surgery from about 1900 until 1977. Dr Bradley-Moore was in general practice here for three decades years and stayed on here in retirement.

The Thatcham Central Cooking Depot

In this age of privatised school meals provision and cafeteria-style services, it is worth recalling how the school meals service originated in this locality. As it happens, Thatcham was particularly important in this respect, because the meals, which were served at many local schools in the district, were supplied from a local kitchen, the Thatcham Central Cooking Depot, in Green Lane.

Historically, school meals are quite a recent innovation. A century ago they were unheard of, although there was clearly a need for them, as a Thatcham news item by 'Josephus' (the pen name of Ambrose White) in the *Newbury Weekly News* in February 1886 shows:

> *Casually meeting children who were returning to school, I was rude enough to ask what they had had for dinner: three told me bread and lard, one bread and dripping and another bread and potatoes.*

These five children were very likely typical of the majority of children in Thatcham – and the country generally – at that time.

In 1906, the then Liberal Government passed the Education (Provision of Meals) Act, under which local authorities were allowed, but not compelled, to make a start with the provision of school meals. However, progress was slow on the whole: school meals were regarded as a form of poor relief and were provided only for undernourished children in 'necessitous districts' – a description which did not apply to an area such as West Berkshire.

Following the outbreak of the Second World War, there was a complete change of policy. In July 1940, with so many mothers working in wartime industries, the Government of the day encouraged local education authorities to provide subsidised meals for as many children as possible, regardless of their parents' incomes. School meals were first provided for Thatcham children at the instigation of Mr Douglas Domoney, headmaster at the local Council School (Francis Baily since 1964) between 1937 and 1962.

Initially, meals were prepared and distributed from the old Bluecoat School building in Chapel Street. Berkshire County Council had leased the building from the trustees since 1917, when – interestingly – it had been used for cookery lessons! In 1942 the building was adapted for use as a cooking depot.

The county council applied for permission to make structural alterations but, as the building is of great historical importance, it is fortunate that these proved to be unnecessary. An existing fireplace and range of cooking equipment were utilised to supply meals to four Thatcham schools. The food was cooked and served by members of the Women's Voluntary Service.

On a national scale, hundreds of school meal centres were constructed during the war years, and in Thatcham a new Central Cooking Depot was built in Green Lane and first supplied hot meals to schools in the district on Monday 29 November 1943. It was a typical wartime austerity building, of breeze-blocks with an asbestos roof and a concrete floor. Inside, equipment included a large refrigerator, fish fryers, six big steam boilers, potato peelers, vegetable shredders and other devices. The food was cooked by heat from a large steam boiler for which a stoker had to be employed at the centre.

In all, the Thatcham Central Cooking Depot employed some 25 personnel. Key staff, of course, were the nine cooks. Among them was Miss Ann McAvey, who came to work at the kitchen soon after it opened. She worked a 10-hour day for the princely sum of £2.10s a week in 1944. Miss McAvey worked at the kitchen until it closed 21 years later. With considerable pride, she well remembered the long hours and hard work she put in at the kitchen.

Staff of the (now demolished) Thatcham Central Cooking Depot in Green Lane – meals for schools in the area were prepared here from 1944–1965.

The cooks arrived at the depot at 5.30a.m. to begin cooking the food. There were porters and a butcher to help them. Every effort was made to offer a varied menu but there was wartime rationing to contend with and a strict budget to adhere to. Each meal cost 8d. (4p) to prepare but was subsidised by the local authority so that the cost to the child was 4d. (2p). Typical meals comprised steak and kidney pie or mince, with potatoes and cabbage, followed by steamed pudding and custard.

At its peak, the depot prepared well over 2,000 meals a day. Food was delivered to schools in metal containers – each of 5, 10 or 20 portions – according to the number of meals the schools required. Thatcham Church of England School took over 100, for instance, but Ashampstead only 10.

The containers were carried to their destinations

by a fleet of half-a-dozen vans that began leaving the depot from about 10.00a.m. onwards. Up to 40 schools were served by the depot including those in places as far away as Aldermaston, Theale, Shinfield, Streatley, Hampstead Norreys and Compton.

During the afternoon the delivery vans returned to the depot with used containers, which had to be washed up. Then there were preparations to be made for the next day's cooking: a normal day might easily call for 4½ cwt of potatoes, 300lbs of meat and 40lbs of dried milk to be got ready, as well as other vegetables and foodstuffs.

Last but by no means least, the kitchen itself had to be thoroughly cleaned before the ladies set out for home at 3.30p.m. Thus the depot was always a hive of industry, and visitors were always impressed with its efficiency, cleanliness and the fine team spirit of the staff.

Cooking Depot staff engaged in painting not cooking during the summer holiday 1946 – included here are Gloria Goodman, Molly Rampton, Anne McAvey and Winnie Ainsworth.

Thatcham's central kitchen operated right through the 1950s and into the 1960s, but by this time schools were having their own individual kitchens built and the demand on the central kitchen declined. In 1961 the depot was only supplying 900 meals to 26 schools and the number was still falling. The depot's days were numbered and the decision was finally taken to close it. After an existence of just over 20 years, the last school meals were prepared there on 23 July 1965.

The central kitchen remained empty for a few years until it was demolished to make way for Crown Court old people's residential home (opened in 1971). Today no trace of the Central Cooking Depot is left, but it served a valuable purpose in its short lifetime. Some of the people who worked there still live in and around Thatcham, whilst countless other West Berkshire residents will surely remember the meals that it provided back in their schooldays.

A Policeman's Lot in Old Thatcham

The provision of police cover in Thatcham was much improved when a new police station was built here. An old charity cottage in Chapel Street (No.20) was sold to Berkshire County Council for £150 in 1904. The cottage was demolished in December of that year and the building of the new police station commenced. It was completed the following summer – it had offices and one cell on the ground floor with living accommodation for a sergeant-in-charge above.

The first officer in charge of Thatcham's police station, from the summer of 1905, was Sgt Daniel Goddard who had a number of men under his control. The value of having a police station, occupied by trained officers, was demonstrated in the spring of 1907, for example, when a motorcyclist met with an 'unfortunate accident' in Chapel Street. He was thrown from his machine and badly injured but Goddard was soon on the spot and 'rendered valuable first aid' whilst awaiting the arrival of a doctor.

Sgt William Gallop succeeded Goddard in November 1911. Gallop was a London man who had trained in Reading and served at both Newbury and Hermitage police stations before taking over at Thatcham. He remained here until 1921, when he moved to Maidenhead. Sergeants then came and went in quick succession during the 1920s: Sgt Harry Brown was succeeded by Sgt Frank Robbins, who was succeeded by Sgt Charles Simmonds.

It was Simmonds who had to deal with a macabre case in November 1929. He was summoned to St Mary's Church by the vicar when two workmen effecting repairs to the belfry discovered a tiny coffin that contained the mummified remains of child who may have been strangled. Simmonds had the coffin conveyed by police car (a sign of further progress in local policing) to the Parish Hall to await an inquest – but that is another story…

After the war, more officers came and went. In the early 1950s, Sgt Anthony Christopher was in charge. Later in the decade it was Sgt Phillip Watts, who was promoted to inspector at Woodley (Reading) in March 1960. During the 1960s, Sgts Charles McGloin, Tudor White and Harold Hawkins each took charge in turn of Thatcham's police station. In November 1967, Sgt Frederick Moore came here, having previously spent four years serving at Bucklebury. He was the last, however – in January 1969, the first panda cars were introduced in the Newbury area and Thatcham's police station was closed later that same year.

The police station stood empty for some time until, in August 1976, it became the office for Thatcham's town council. In 1984 the council moved to new premises and the police moved back in on a part-time basis, but it's still a far cry from what things used to be like.

Some years ago, there were still retired police officers in Thatcham who were pleased to recall their memories of a 'policeman's lot' at the old village police station, as it used to be. They included Mr John Giles, an ex-regular officer, and Messrs Maurice Lane and Hubert Hawkins, both ex-war reserve officers stationed there during the Second World War.

Mr Giles, who in retirement lived in Park Lane, came from a family once associated with Newbury. His grandfather ran a bakery business in Cheap Street, close to the railway station. His father, Mr Leighton Giles, joined the old Berkshire County Police in 1902 – at which date his pay was 19s.10d. per week, a far cry indeed from today!

Because his father was then serving as a sergeant at Arborfield, that is where Mr Giles was born. His father served with the Berkshire police for 37 years, moving across the county and finally being promoted to superintendent at Abingdon. Mr Giles himself joined the Berkshire Constabulary in 1932 and served at various towns as far afield as Ascot, Faringdon, Wantage and Maidenhead.

A few years after joining the force, PC Giles did special duty at Windsor on 28 January 1936, for the funeral of King George V. Like other officers on duty that day, he was later presented with a black-edged certificate to mark the occasion.

In 1942 PC Giles was stationed at Brimpton, within the Thatcham section of the county force. His beat encompassed a large area round about including Greenham, Crookham, Woolhampton and Bucklebury. In order to police this large area effectively, he became one of Berkshire's early motorcycle

officers – his first machine was a 500c.c. 'Rudge'. The war was then on and his duties at that time were mainly concerned with the movements of the 3,000 servicemen and 1,000 vehicles arriving at Greenham Common as America entered the conflict.

He has fond memories of Thatcham's police station during the war years, and recalled how Sgt Alfred Walker established a clubroom there. Mr Giles pointed out that the clubroom was not only for police officers but was also open to members of the Auxiliary Fire Brigade, Civil Defence Corps and Home Guard.

An amusing story is told about Thatcham's police station as it was in 1940. At that time it had a platform fixed on its roof to hold an air-raid siren. One summer morning a stranger, passing through the village, chanced to look up and see the platform – not knowing what it was, it struck him as resembling an altana (a platform characteristically found on the roofs of Venetian houses). Just then the local sergeant – '12 stones of ruddy British beef' – rode up on his bicycle, followed by his dog. 'I'm interested to see you've an altana', said the stranger. 'No, sir, she's a red setter', replied the sergeant thinking it was the dog, not the platform, to which the stranger had referred.

During this period, Thatcham's police station was staffed by up to four dozen men including regular officers, war reserves and special constables. The officer-in-charge at this time was Sgt Alfred Walker, who came to Thatcham from Maidenhead and afterwards went to Hungerford as an Inspector, subsequently being promoted to Superintendent.

During the Second World War, other emergency services shared Thatcham's police station clubroom. Seen here in August 1943 are the village's ARP Rescue Services personnel, set up by 'Squire' A.S.B. Tull (seated centre).

As a sergeant, Alfred Walker is remembered as 'firm but fair'. He was born at Lichfield in Staffordshire and liked to talk about his home town, especially its fine cathedral; his officers regarded him as 'an educated man'.

The impact that American servicemen, stationed at Greenham, had on Thatcham – then a small village – brought back memories. In off-duty hours the Americans frequented public houses in Thatcham and the Wheatsheaf appears to have been one of their favourite haunts. This proved most convenient for the village bobbies, who only had to walk across the road when they were required (as, it seems, they often were) to 'persuade' some Americans to leave at closing time. On their way back to the base, the Americans usually stopped off at the Chapel Street fish and chip shop (then kept by Aubrey Collins), which did a roaring trade.

There were eight regular officers in the Thatcham police section in the postwar years, these being a sergeant and two constables at Thatcham, two constables at Hermitage, and one constable each at Yattendon, Bucklebury and Brimpton. When not on duty, the Thatcham sergeant (and one of the constables, PC Mugford, who lived opposite the Plough in London Road) were on call at all times.

During the postwar years, PC Giles undertook a full range of police duties. From dealing with the 'pranks' of village 'lads', through burglaries and house-breakings, to drownings in the River Kennet and fatalities on the Bath Road – it was all part of a policeman's lot. Mr Giles retired from the force in 1963 and was awarded a long-service medal in recognition of his 31 years' service with the Berkshire Constabulary.

Mr Lane, who in retirement lived in Bath Road, was born in Chapel Street, close to the old police station, in 1908. He spent his working life at Colthrop Mill except for the war years when he served with the War Reserve Police. He was based throughout at Thatcham police station and has vivid memories of 'point duty' at the top of the Broadway. Here, the task of passing convoys of military vehicles round the tight bends proved a considerable challenge, especially the long glider trailers.

On at least two occasions, PC Lane apprehended German POWs who had escaped from detention. He captured two Germans at Woolhampton after they had escaped from a POW camp at Ascot, and took them into custody at Thatcham. He helped to arrest others, spotted on the railway line at Colthrop – when he questioned them, it turned out that they had hoped to follow the railway to Bristol and then escape in a boat. More macabre incidents were recalled by Mr Lane who said that if there was a body to be found then he 'usually seemed to be the officer who discovered it'.

Both Mr Lane and Mr Hawkins recalled doing turns of duty at Bowdown House on Greenham Common during the period when King Haakon of Norway resided there. The police officers responsible for the monarch's protection were issued with Colt revolvers but only had five rounds of ammunition – 'it seemed stupid to me', commented Mr Hawkins.

Fortunately nothing untoward ever happened, although he recollected being on duty there one night with a rather nervous PC from Newbury. When – in the darkness – a flight of swans passed over, the Newbury officer panicked, thinking that German paratroopers were landing, but Mr Hawkins was able to dissuade him from raising the alarm.

Mr Lane and Mr Hawkins remember a great deal about their time with the War Reserve Police in Thatcham. They recollect the old police station quite clearly. Of its single cell, Mr Lane thought that it was not much used to detain local felons – instead, Sgt Walker used it as a quiet retreat 'to catch up on his paperwork'. Of the air-raid siren, Mr Hawkins recalled that he had 'switched it on many a time', after a red-alert was phoned through from Newbury.

Mr Hawkins, who in retirement lived at Gilbert Court, was born at Fairoak Farm, Ashford Hill, in 1902. He spent his early working life in farming but after the Second World War broke out came to live in Thatcham in 1940 and joined the War Reserve Police. For the duration of the war, he undertook normal police work and saw duty at Southampton and Portsmouth during air raids and at other difficult times.

'It wasn't always so grim', chuckled Mr Hawkins, as he recalled an episode in which four American soldiers in a jeep asked him for directions. He was cycling past the Swan pub in London Road when the jeep – 'on the wrong side of the road' – screeched to a halt in front of him. The Captain driving the vehicle called out 'How far is it to Marlborough?'.

As the Americans were driving in the wrong direction for Marlborough, PC Hawkins decided to 'have a bit of fun with them'. He called back 'it's about 25,000 miles, give or take a few'. The soldiers' mouths dropped open in amazement, at which the PC added 'but it's only 20 miles if you go that way', pointing back towards Newbury.

Of his joke, Mr Hawkins says, 'it was well worth it', but he declined to repeat what the soldiers called him when it dawned on them what he meant by his answer.

Mr Hawkins, who began his career with the War Reserve Police in 1940, joined the Berkshire county police when the war ended in 1945. He was given just two weeks' training and was then appointed a regular officer, receiving a full police pay of £8–10s. per week. For this, the work was often arduous and the hours were anti-social, involving both night work and 'split-shifts'.

The Thatcham officers, such as PC Hawkins, also had a wide area to patrol. As their tour of duty took them well into the surrounding countryside, a bicycle

Thatcham's purpose-built police station was located in Chapel Street and was first occupied during the summer of 1905; it is seen here around that date.

The top of the Broadway, looking west into the High Street in the 1930s – Mr Lane had vivid memories of doing 'point duty' here around this time, passing vehicles round the tight bends.

An early view of Greenham Common where PCs Lane and Hawkins recalled doing turns of duty in the Second World War when King Haakon of Norway lived here in exile at Bowdown House.

Thatcham's police officers – regular, war reserves and special constables – photographed at Turnfields in about 1942. Among them are war reserve constables Fred Stark, Neville Lawrence and Maurice Lane (middle row, fifth, sixth and seventh from left respectively). In the front row (on chairs) are Thatcham's Sgt Walker and Newbury's Superintendent Lambourne (sixth and seventh from right respectively).

was essential. In the course of an eight-hour shift, a constable was expected to be at four 'points' (each one a phone box) by a particular time, so that Newbury Headquarters could ring him up if necessary.

In Thatcham itself, 'all the shop doors were inspected every night', recalls Mr Hawkins, 'and the unoccupied houses visited'.

After a 12-year career as a regular officer, Mr Hawkins retired from the police force in 1957. He recalls one incident especially with some amusement. This was in March 1954, when a Guinness tanker failed to negotiate the double bend at the top of the Broadway and overturned outside the White Hart. The building was badly damaged and its cellar was flooded with nearly 1000 gallons of stout from the stricken tanker.

As the officer sent to deal with the accident, PC Hawkins found that he had his hands full. He had to turn off the gas and dowse a fire inside the pub, arrange a traffic diversion in the street outside, and search the building to see if anyone was buried in the debris. (In the event, there were no casualties as it was closing time and the few customers left on the premises were in the toilet at the other end of the building).

To make things more difficult, a crowd began to gather. Assistance was afforded from an unexpected quarter, however. Some of the stout from the tanker ran into the gutter where several dogs began to lap it up. 'Needless to say they were soon drunk, just like people', laughed Mr Hawkins. 'When they tried to walk they fell over their own feet – it certainly amused the crowd and helped to keep them out of my way'. Looking back, he thought it had been 'quite funny' – who says a policeman's lot is not a happy one?

In March 1954 a Guinness tanker failed to negotiate the Broadway corner and crashed into the White Hart. PC Hawkins was the officer who had to deal with the incident.

Chapter III
Long-gone Village Schools

The History of a Thatcham Charity School

Thatcham's charity school was housed in a four-teenth century chapel which had lain empty for 150 years until Lady Frances Winchcombe of Bucklebury purchased the ruined building and the land on which it stood – reputedly for a mere 10s. (50p) – in the early-eighteenth century. By a trust deed dated June 1707, she directed that the building be converted into a 'schoolhouse' for the education of 30 poor boys from Bucklebury, Thatcham and Little Shefford, to include 'religious instruction in accordance with the doctrines of the Church of England'.

Lady Winchcombe also gave money to pay the running costs of the school: the schoolmaster's salary (£20), apprenticeships for 3 boys (£20), the purchase of Bibles and 'other useful books' (£l0), repairs to the building (£2) and an annual dinner (£1). She appointed seven trustees to run the school after her death, which occurred later in 1707, but for nearly 90 years the trustees proved incompetent. The trustees only opened the school at all after legal proceedings had been taken against them (and then not until 1713) and after their deaths the school closed in 1730.

By a decree of the Court of Chancery dated 26 July 1793, the charity school was reopened with effect from 24 June 1794, under schoolmaster John Blay on a salary of £50 a year. From this date the school became known as the Bluecoat School from the uniform worn by the boys, which consisted of beaver hats, blue coats, blue stockings and yellow leather breeches. The boys' uniforms were provided for them and issued annually on the anniversary day of the school's reopening. The lessons consisted of reading, writing and 'casting accounts' (arithmetic).

The relatively low salary made it difficult to recruit teachers for the school. However, in 1807 William Harris became the schoolmaster – on the same salary

A close-up of the Bluecoat School building in 1985 – at this date it was being used as an antiques shop, but even after nearly seven centuries still showed evidence of its days as a chapel.

– and taught here for 47 years In 1819 a report of the Charity Commissioners found that 40 boys were being clothed and educated at the school; by using the 'Madras' (monitorial) system, Mr Blay was also able to teach a further 40–50 boys, for which he was paid an extra ten guineas a year – raised by public subscription – and at this date 5 or 6 boys a year were found apprenticeships at a cost to the charity of £10.

In May, 1855, Edwin Head was appointed schoolmaster at a salary of £52 a year; he must have been a good teacher, as his salary was increased to £56 in 1861 and £60 a year in 1862. In 1864 the trustees deposited £200 with the Newbury Savings Bank with a view to providing him with a house and in 1869 the accumulated fund was used towards purchasing a plot of land next to the school from Loundyes' Charity for £340, and a schoolmaster's residence was built by 1870. The annual mid-summer dinner was still held, usually in the assembly room of the New Inn.

The school was then subject to inspection by the Oxford Diocesan Inspection of Schools: that of 1891 reported that Thatcham's charity school 'continued to be very carefully instructed'. The number of pupils on the roll fluctuated by this time – in 1896 it was 39 but by 1899 it was only 26. The boys were often seen being marched to the Parish Church for services, with their master following at the rear. Called 'Little Head' from his stature, he was nevertheless well-respected although getting on in years (he served the school for 46 years, up to his death in 1901).

As his health declined, he was placed on reduced salary and given an assistant teacher – James Whiddett – from March 1900. The latter became schoolmaster in turn, serving until November 1909, when he was succeeded by Frederick Carter, who only stayed at the school for nine months. George James Fyfield then filled the vacancy as temporary master for a few months, prior to the appointment of Samuel Vallis as the village's Bluecoat schoolmaster from October 1910.

When war broke out in 1914, the school closed 'for the duration' and Samuel Vallis enlisted in the army. During the war, the school was taken over for military purposes but never reopened as a school after the war. By 1926 Thatcham Parish Council decided to refer its unsatisfactory administration to the Charity Commissioners, urging that if the provisions of the endowment were not carried out that an alternative scheme should be set up. This was effected as of October that year, with Councillors J.M. Henry and T.H. Brown being appointed as extra charity trustees.

The new scheme split the charity into two foundations (one relating to Thatcham, the other to East Shefford) and directed that Thatcham's Bluecoat School should be discontinued, the charity's income instead being applied in various ways, including the teaching of religious education in local church schools. In this respect, grants totalling £90 a year were made to Church of England schools at Thatcham (£45), Cold Ash (£23) and Bucklebury (£22), both for the maintenance of their premises and for religious instruction in accordance with the wishes of the charity's founder.

In 1931, Cllr Brown (as a trustee and staunch Nonconformist) challenged the grant to Thatcham's Church of England School on the grounds that the religious instruction being given at the school involved the pupils' attendance at Parish Church services where 'high church' rites were 'taught and practised'. The matter was referred to the Board of Education but it decided that there was no reason to deny the grant to Thatcham's C. of E. School and so payments continued on the same basis as before. Grants to local church schools for other purposes were also permitted under the 1926 scheme.

During the Second World War, the old Bluecoat School building was used for the preparation of meals for local schools and in the postwar years as an 'annexe' where woodwork and cookery lessons were

The view east along Chapel Street around 1900 showing the Bluecoat School, located in the old chapel of the borough; Marsh House (demolished in 1972) can also be seen (left).

The old chapel seen from the south-east – by this time it was derelict but still showed signs of its one time ecclesiastical use with the priests' door in the south wall.

The view east along Chapel Street in 1985 – Marsh House (left) *has now disappeared, and even the New Inn/Prancing Horse* (right) *is no longer a pub, but Thatcham's second oldest building still stands* (centre).

taught. By the late 1960s, the building had been disused for several years and subject to vandalism. Its future was discussed at Thatcham Parish Council meetings. Opinion was divided but one councillor called it 'a monstrosity' – another agreed, adding: 'Our grandchildren would not say thank you for this building'. It was a 'traffic hazard' and councillors wanted it removed!

Under the terms of a 'vesting declaration' in 1969 the trustees of the old Bluecoat School agreed to sell it for £2,500 to Newbury District Council. NDC allocated £5,800 for the acquisition, site and repair work – which was completed in 1974 – and offered to lease it to Thatcham Town Council to convert into an 'art gallery-museum'. For some time to come, however, it was leased for retail purposes, being occupied by an antiques dealer for many years, before passing via the town council into the hands of a charitable trust, formed in 2005, which will return it to public use.

The funds from Lady Winchcombe's endowment continue to provide an income for grants to Sunday schools and young people beginning training or commencing further education after leaving school. To meet the requirements of the Sex Discrimination Act, a scheme dating from 1981 has included girls in the charity, which is now administered by 11 trustees (five council nominations, three incumbents plus three co-optees), serving four-year terms. Like Thatcham's other charity trustee bodies, that of the Lady Winchcombe Charity has been chaired by David Wootton since 1982.

Memories of a Bluecoat Schoolboy

In an interview some years ago, Mr Stanley Eggleton afforded a valuable insight into the daily life of a pupil at Thatcham's Bluecoat School. Born in 1902, his family came to live at Bucklebury, where he attended the village school until he was nine years old. Then, in 1911, his parents applied for him to be admitted to this charity school and he was taken there by his mother to face a 'selection procedure' before the schoolmaster (Mr Vallis), along with the vicar (Revd Edward Chamberlain), the 'Squire' (Mr A. R. Tull) and Mr G. J. Fyfield.

'We had to do some reading in front of these gentlemen there while they took notes', remembered Mr Eggleton. 'We also had to do a bit of writing and spelling and that kind of thing'. The whole thing took 'quite a while' but as a result he was admitted to the school that year. The school catered for the boys

39

of Thatcham and Bucklebury but as there was no school transport at that date all the pupils walked to school, including those from the outlying village.

In bad weather the boys' clothing got wet on the way to school so they had to engage in 'warm up' activities whilst Mr Vallis played such music as the William Tell Overture on the harmonium! Heating in the schoolroom came from a large tortoiseshell stove – the older boys had to fill the coke scuttles from which it was fuelled. Any pupils who had been punished with the cane during the day also had the job of cleaning it out before going home in the evening.

Sometimes Mr Vallis would ask the boys 'Who's got a pocket knife?'. When an unsuspecting victim answered 'I have, Sir', the boy would be told to go and cut the teacher a stick 'over the flouse' – the ditch alongside Dunstan Green. When he returned with the stick, the boy was usually the first of many that day to get a blow from it. 'We got the cane for misbehaviour, trivial things,' remembered Mr Eggleton, and 'us small boys were afraid to do anything'.

The school day started with assembly, 'then you took scripture lessons and things like that'. There was a half-hour break during the morning and then two hours for lunch, from midday to 2.00p.m. The teacher would spend lunchtime gardening or engaged in some other business at his house, Bluecoats, or in the New Inn across the road, leaving the boys to their own devices. If the weather was fine, the boys played on the green but if it was bad, they stayed in the school.

At that time, horses and ponies roamed freely on The Marsh and drovers passed by on the road. 'Some of the lads out in the street might torment the old drovers when they came through' – if the drovers then chased them, the boys would run to the school and try to blockade themselves in to avoid getting their ears boxed. Other boys were content to play in the street, with tops or hoops, 'because there was hardly any traffic then'.

The boys sometimes ventured as far as the Broadway where they sat on the seat around the cross, or they would watch Mr Shepherd, the village tailor, making their uniforms in his shop. The boys were supplied with a uniform annually: it consisted of a blue three-quarter length coat, corduroy trousers and a pillbox hat. They were also issued with hobnailed boots which were supplied by Mr Tucker who had a shoe shop in the Broadway.

The premises of the tailor, Joseph Shepherd, are now an off-licence but in those days the Bluecoat boys 'used to go and line up sometimes and peep in the window' to see him making their uniforms. ' That was the only suit you had for the year. You only had to wear that on a Sunday when you went to church, not in the week, until you got the next one'.

On 'high days' or 'church days', the Bluecoat boys had to march up from their school to the Parish Church for a service. 'If any of us lads had a good voice for singing, we had to go in the choir', recalled Mr Eggleton. 'That was in the week, of course'. Today, it is difficult to imagine the sound the boys' hobnailed boots made as – led by Mr Vallis – they marched along Chapel Street and down the Broadway on their way to St Mary's Church.

When the First World War broke out in 1914, the Bluecoat School effectively closed because Mr Vallis, being a national reservist, was 'called up'. The boys at the school were then dispersed to other local

Left: *The Bluecoat School seen from the east in the early years of the twentieth century – the boys standing in the road may be Bluecoat schoolboys. Chapel Street can be seen beyond the school.*

Far left: *A rare close-up photograph of a Bluecoat schoolboy around 1900. The uniform consisted of blue coats and leather breeches – the latter were very uncomfortable to sit in when dried hastily after a soaking in the rain!*

The Bluecoat School seen from the west in the early years of the twentieth century – the boys lined up in front of the building are some of those who attended the school at this time, as did Stan Eggleton.

Church of England schools able to accommodate them. Some went to the National School in Park Lane but Mr Eggleton was transferred to St Mark's School at Cold Ash. 'I think it was about two years after that I left school', he remembered.

By 1980, there were only a few ex-Bluecoat schoolboys still alive in Thatcham. 'I think there's only six of us left alive now', recalled Mr Eggleton. 'All the rest have passed away'. The others still living in Thatcham then included Jimmy Hanson, Ernie Arnold, Reg Wise and Reg Greenhough. Since that time, even they have passed on and, sadly, Stanley Eggleton himself died on 3 March 1986, but fortunately his memories remain with us.

Miss Marjorie Brown's Prep School

Miss Marjorie Brown's Preparatory School began operating in Thatcham after the First World War. A daughter of Mr and Mrs Arthur Brown of Wetherdene, a house in Park Lane, Miss Brown was educated at Newbury High School and Cheltenham Ladies' College, where she was trained according to the pioneering Froebel principles of education.

It was not until the twentieth century that schools in this country began to use what had become known as the 'New Teaching'. Having qualified as a schoolmistress, Marjorie Brown taught at several private schools in the Middlesex area before returning to Thatcham to set up her own venture.

Miss Brown lived with her parents at Wetherdene. It was her father who paid to have a small schoolhouse built in the (then) meadow belonging to the Brown family on the opposite side of the road. The schoolhouse fronted Park Lane, having a stable, shed and toilet (with wooden seat and bucket) behind.

This preparatory school opened in 1923 and, as a private establishment, charged fees; the amount is not known but may have been about £5 per term. It was a 'mixed' school and normally had up to 15 boys and girls – aged from 5 to 11 years – on the roll at any one time. Miss Brown did all the teaching herself.

The building was entered through a porch, which had a little cloakroom on the left – the pupils' paintings were usually pinned up here. Built of brick, its internal walls were wood-lined and not painted but stained a dark green colour. There was a tortoiseshell stove to provide heating in the schoolhouse.

Pupils sat at twin desks, which had lift-up lids and inkwells, although not much writing was done in ink. They wrote in double-lined exercise books and had readers such as *Old Lob the Farmer* – very appropriate in a rural location like Thatcham! They even had woodwork lessons, in which they used fretsaws.

Miss Brown was an accomplished pianist and so there was much singing. The musical life of the school extended to putting on public concerts at the British School in Church Lane to raise funds for Dr Barnardo's. The pupils wore costumes for performances – the girls once dressed up as 'Flower Fairies'.

The exterior of Miss Brown's Prep School building, photographed just prior to its demolition.

The interior of Miss Brown's Prep School, looking towards what was the original entrance door.

Pupils outside Thatcham's 'prep' school, c.1935. Left to right: Rob Brown, John Brown, Mary Lay, Denise Brown, Peter Brown, Ursula Jackson, David Morrison, Donald Robbins.

Pupils from the school 'crocodile' down Park Lane on their way to 'pond-dipping' near St Mary's Church, led by Gordon Barr (white shirt, shorts), with Marjorie Brown (left) and Mrs A. Brown (right) at the rear.

School began at 9.00a.m. and lessons included the 3Rs. In arithmetic lessons, pupils used foot rulers with imperial units on the front and centimetres on the back. Studying the back of his ruler one day, a pupil asked Miss Brown what 'mms' were. 'They're foreign', she replied, 'we don't bother with those'!

All the pupils went home at lunchtime. At the end of the day Miss Brown read the pupils a story. They sat round her in a circle on seats arranged in a pecking order by age, from an hour-glass basket chair for the oldest, through other chairs and basket stools, down to hard wooden stools for the youngest.

In keeping with her Froebel principles, Miss Brown took her pupils on many delightful walks around Thatcham. A favourite with many was to inspect the flint-lined Roman well, then recently discovered in a private garden at Bourne Arch. Another treat was 'pond-dipping', where Meadow Close is now.

At the end of a term, each pupil was allowed to select a gramophone record to be played – one young lady's favourite was 'The Laughing Policeman'. At the end of

the academic year, there was an annual picnic in 'Granny Brown's Orchard'. This was part of the school grounds; 'Granny' being Mrs Arthur Brown.

Many local people were pupils at Miss Brown's school before going on to high schools in Newbury and elsewhere. Thatcham's 'prep' school finally shut down in August 1951, after a life of 28 years, and Miss Brown retired – she never married and died in 1972. A modern housing development now stands in the meadow where the school – demolished in 2005 – once stood.

Thatcham's British School: A Postscript

Although it is still known by the name, the British School in Thatcham has not functioned as such for nearly a century. At one time, of course, there were elderly residents in the village who had attended the school as children and who could remember their schooldays there. One of them was Mrs Margaret Sharpe. She was born Margaret Tigwell, in Thatcham, on Christmas Day 1896. Her family (who were Plymouth Brethren) lived in Station Road, at Spring Cottages (demolished in 1982 to make way for the Moors Relief Road).

Prior to the First World War, between the ages of 5 and 14 – from 1902 until 1911, just a couple of years before it closed – she was a pupil at the British School in Church Lane. She began in the infant section of the school. The infants were taught in 'the little room' at the back of the school and worked not in books but on slates.

Mrs Sharpe was taught by infant teacher Miss Rhoda Pearce and remembered her as a rather bad-tempered teacher! At this date there were only about 30 pupils in the infant class but Miss Pearce had two younger teachers – Miss Eleanor Pinnock and Miss Hettie Peters – to assist her.

Later, Mrs Sharpe transferred to the senior section of the school. Here she was taught by Mr Horatio Skillman. Standing behind his big desk, Mr Skillman always had his cane 'at the ready'. Boys were caned frequently and girls occasionally – Mrs Sharpe remembered being caned on the hand once for talking during a lesson.

Nevertheless, the teaching was quite effective. The pupils were grouped into 'standards' and their lessons consisted of the customary 3Rs – reading, writing and 'rithmetic. Mrs Sharpe's favourite lessons were poetry (she was still able to recite some of the lines she learned in her schooldays) and needlework. The needlework lessons were still taught by Miss Pearce: like all schoolgirls then, Mrs Sharpe had to make a 'sampler', which she kept for many years after leaving school.

Looking back on her schooldays, Mrs Sharpe readily admitted that she 'couldn't wait to leave'. What she

St Mary's Church in about 1911, as Maggie Sharpe (née Tigwell) would have known it – that was the year she finished her education at the British School in Church Lane behind St Mary's.

The view south down Church Lane c.1900, past the British School and Independent Church (left).

A photograph showing the children of Standard IV at the old British School in Church Lane before the First World War – Maggie Sharpe (née Tigwell) can be seen in the front row (left).

liked best was the companionship: the school day was from 9a.m. to 3.45p.m., with an hour for lunch in the middle of the day. Although she did not live very far away, she liked to bring sandwiches to school and eat them in the playground with her friends.

Even though she had no great love of school, Mrs Sharpe attended faithfully until she completed her compulsory education in 1911 and left to go 'into service'. Upon leaving, she was awarded a regular attendance medal inscribed with her name – 'Maggie Tigwell' – and recording the fact that she was 'Never Absent, Never Late' at the British School, Thatcham. Mrs Sharpe's photograph shows her – as Maggie Tigwell (*front row, left*) – in Standard IV. Most of the other children in the group can be identified but they represent a generation no longer with us today. Sadly, some of the boys were killed just a few years after the photograph was taken, as soldiers in the First World War.

From Old School to New School

At Easter 1913, some Thatcham schoolchildren prepared to transfer from their old school to a new school. Easter Sunday was on 23 March that year, and these children finished their spring term at one school before going back to another to commence their summer term. The old school was the British School in Church Lane whilst the new one was the Council School (now Francis Baily) in London Road, Thatcham.

The British School had opened in 1847 to cater for the children of the village's nonconformists. After many trials and tribulations, the school became the most successful in the village, largely under the leadership of Mr Horatio Barton Skillman, headmaster from March, 1882. He proved to be a competent and popular teacher, being presented with the gift of a microscope by old scholars to mark his 21st year at the school in 1903.

However, in 1910, HM Inspectors informed the school's managers that it no longer met the requirements of the Education Department. A new playground was urgently needed and the managers were informed that it would cost up to £500 to provide one. The managers replied that they could not raise the money and the county council declined to take the school over owing to the limited potential of the Church Lane site.

Berkshire County Council decided Thatcham should have a new school instead and plans were made to close the old British School. Its last day of operation as a public 'elementary school' was (Maundy) Thursday 20 March 1913. Scholars and teachers alike took an 'affectionate farewell' of the old building. The teachers in particular – most of whom had worked there 'with distinction' for many years – found leaving 'quite a wrench'.

Pupils at the British School in Church Lane were photographed here in about 1900 with Mr H. B. Skillman (headmaster from 1882 to 1913 when this school closed – he transferred to the Council School and was headmaster there until 1922).

Thatcham's old British School opened in 1847 and is seen here in about 1914 – the wall and railings in front of the playground were removed after it ceased to be a school.

The Council School, photographed sometime around 1920 with pupils in its playground – the turret on top of the building housed a bell, used to summon the children to school.

The new purpose-built Council School, which first opened its doors to pupils on Tuesday 1 April 1913 – at that time it was judged to be 'a splendid building'.

A group of older pupils at the Council School pose for the photographer around 1920 – when the school opened a few years earlier some 200 children enrolled, most transferring from the British School.

As the spring term drew to a close, a special children's concert was staged to say farewell to the old school. It had been proposed to stage two performances, on the afternoon and evening of the penultimate day of term (Wednesday) but such was the 'crush' at the evening performance – the schoolroom being packed before the advertised start time and large numbers being turned away – the show was repeated on the Thursday evening.

The programme was 'of a high class character' featuring excellent singing, the action songs being performed with a 'smartness and precision' which 'demonstrated careful and thorough training'. The items were varied – 'adding additional interest and pleasure' – with the infants performing during the first half and the older pupils during the second half. The pupils started by singing two choruses, 'England' and 'Now We Pray'.

A sign of the times, one of the older girls (Vera Holdup) was dressed as Britannia in white robe and scarlet cloak, with a brass helmet and plume, holding a trident and shield covered with a Union flag. She was seated on a dais, dressed with a similar flag, and next to her stood 'lads dressed in Navy costume. Around and behind her were the rest of the pupils, some holding miniature flags – a very pleasing and effective scene to behold'.

Meanwhile, the Council School was nearing completion along the London Road. The choice of location for the new school proved controversial, and had not been considered suitable by everyone in the village. It was constructed by George Elms (Builders) of Marsh Benham at a cost of £4,000. Over the Easter holiday large numbers of people visited the new school, evidently being impressed and offering many 'expressions of admiration'.

General opinion was that the contrast with the old school was very striking. The Council School was judged 'a splendid building', making the British School appear 'more prison-like than ever'! This, it was argued, would help 'prejudice against the position' to wear off. Indeed, objectors to the location of the new school were soon won over, now that it was finished and its surroundings could be appreciated 'in the proper perspective'.

The school stood some distance away from the main road, from which the 'best' side of the building could not be seen. 'This is as it should be', it was said, 'and gives all the classrooms a south-easterly or south-westerly aspect with beautiful expansive views' (at that date, the view was across cornfields). Outside the school were large gravelled playgrounds – which had been well drained – and also 'a good-sized shelter'.

There were five classrooms: three to hold 48 pupils each plus two for the infants (one for 42, another for 30). They were arranged along an L-shaped corridor opposite cloakrooms, lavatories, a storeroom and teachers' room. The classrooms had block wood floors to lessen noise, being well equipped with scholastic furniture and cupboard space. The blackboards were not on easels but fixtures, made from 'a composition of glass'.

Like the rest of the school, the classrooms were well lit and ventilated. The whole building was heated by hot water pipes on a system claimed to be 'perfect'. The school had its own 'capital water supply obtained from an artesian well'. All in all, everything about the new Council School seemed to be 'arranged for comfort and safety' – as the start of the summer term loomed, it would soon be time to open its doors to the pupils.

Thatcham's new purpose-built public elementary school was ready to receive its first pupils at the start of the summer term, 1913. Known as the Council School, it was located on a greenfield site out along the London Road and up to 200 children trooped to and fro there every school day. It first opened its doors on Tuesday 1 April 1913.

The teachers who awaited them that day had transferred *en masse* from the old British School. The headmaster was Mr H. B. Skillman, assisted by Miss 'Hettie' Peters (Certificated), Miss Eleanor Pinnock (Uncertificated), Miss Rhoda Pearce and Miss Kate Ashman (both Supplementary), along with a young newcomer, Miss Mayors (Monitoress).

Appointed as the school's first managers were Councillor T.H. Brown and Mrs Charlotte Carter, members of two well-known Thatcham families. The school's first caretaker was not a local man, however, but hailed from Dorset – he was Mr A. Chalker of Weymouth, a Royal Navy pensioner who had retired with the rank of Chief Petty Officer.

Within days, the school had filled all its places, with over 190 pupils on the roll. It soon became necessary to appoint a further teacher and an assistant master was sought, to start at Whitsun. As an interim measure, however, a Mr Cross of Bracknell Council School, stepped into the breach at the start of May, and stayed on here for some time.

Thatcham's Council School soon got into its stride under such an experienced staff. Mr Skillman, the headmaster, is remembered by one ex-pupil as 'a much-loved, if somewhat fiery, little man'. He certainly seems to have run the school effectively and it is no surprise therefore that it received a good report when subjected to its first inspection.

HM Inspectors first visited the school on Friday 20 June 1913. They acknowledged that the school had only been opened since April and were pleased to find that its 'work was well in hand'. The pupils throughout the school were described as 'bright and attentive' and the lessons were said to be 'given with earnestness and interest'.

Overall, the village's new Council School had 'made a very good start', and so things continued. Following the summer holiday (and harvest), Thatcham's 'day schools' reopened for their autumn term on Monday 15 September 1913. Council School teachers resumed their work; interestingly, it is known that two of them had a love of local history!

Not surprisingly, therefore, pupils were taken on 'nature rambles' around the village. A favourite walk took them up to the site of the former Dunston House, opposite the school. As autumn gave way to winter, the pupils gathered on the school playground to create 'the longest slide' they could on the ice that had formed there on 'crisp mornings'.

Inside, Mr Chalker stoked up the boilers to warm the school and heat was circulated all round the building through the 'perfect' piped hot water system. That was not the only thing to do so: it was recalled by an ex-pupil that Miss Rhoda Pearce had a very loud voice which – 'when raised in ungentle admonition' – was heard all over the school!

As the New Year of 1914 began, no-one could foresee just how eventful it would turn out to be. Perhaps some of the very lads who had dressed in Navy costume to appear in the children's concert which marked the closure of the British School less than a year earlier would eventually wear a real uniform before the First World War finished.

In the postwar years, there were some staff changes at the Council School. Sadly, Rhoda Pearce died on 20 June 1921, having been 'for 30 years a teacher of little children in this village'. Buried in the cemetery near to the school, her grave has a memorial erected by 'past and present' teachers and scholars of the British and Council Schools.

Having reached the age limit imposed by the Education Authority, Mr Skillman was obliged to retire as the Council School's headmaster on 31 December 1922. A retirement ceremony was held for him and his wife Salatina at the old British School in March 1923, at which he was presented with a wallet containing the sum of £52.10s.

Over 400 of his former pupils had subscribed towards his gift. Some were present at the meeting where speeches were made as a tribute to the 40 years' educational service Mr Skillman had given to the community. One of his ex-pupil teachers – William Mathews – spoke appreciatively of 'the good tone of the school' whilst in his charge.

Council School manager, Mr T.H. Brown, described him as 'a good man, a good master and thoroughly interested in the best welfare of each and all of his scholars'. Mr Skillman returned to his hometown of Burton Bradstock, Dorset, where he died aged 85 on 5 November 1943. He was one of Thatcham's most highly respected schoolmasters.

A group of infant children (aged between five and seven) at the Council School pose for the photographer with teachers Miss Rhoda Pearce (left) and her niece Miss Minnie Pearce (right) in March 1920.

Chapter IV

Schools with a History

A History of St Mary's School

Thatcham's first Church of England school, built in the Broadway with the help of a £50 grant from the National Society, was opened in 1828. However, it soon became oversubscribed – it was taking in 140 children a day within 15 years – so the village's Anglicans planned a new school. Mr Vincent Clementi, the curate at St Mary's Church, applied for further grants from the National Society and the Government's Education Committee. The former body granted £150 and the latter £180 towards the construction of a new school building.

In November 1844, Mr William Mount of Wasing donated an acre of waste land at Clapper's green, on the east side of Park Lane as a site for the new school, which was built during 1845 at a cost of almost £900, to accommodate 300 local boys and girls. Known as 'St Mary's', it opened its doors in 1846. The first

The Church of England National School (St Mary's) in Park Lane – built during 1845 at a cost of £900, the school could accommodate 300 pupils and had a schoolmaster's house adjoining it (right).

The view north up Park Lane in the 1930s – St Mary's School is on the right in the distance.

headmaster and headmistress at St Mary's were William Botterill and his wife Caroline Botterill. In 1850 Edwin Head became headmaster at St Mary's School but in 1855 he moved on to become headmaster at the Bluecoat School.

Samuel Vallis senr was appointed headmaster of St Mary's School in 1855 and served as such for 12 years. He lived in the schoolhouse built on the premises and his son Samuel Vallis junr was born here in 1856. The latter eventually became a pupil-teacher at the school before entering Culham Training College in 1873; he later returned to Thatcham, a qualified schoolmaster himself. Samuel Vallis junr was headmaster of St Mary's from 1878–1880 but the years following his father's headship were an unsettled period for the school.

In three decades from 1867–1898 St Mary's was served by no fewer than a dozen headmasters – in 1877 alone, three headmasters came and went – and for the whole of the autumn term of 1897 the school was closed completely, apparently on account of 'fever'! Then, in 1898 George Waite was appointed headmaster and gave 14 years' service in this capacity. However, even he had a difficult time at the school – following an unsatisfactory inspection by HMI in 1912 Mr Waite resigned from the post in the summer of that same year.

During the academic year 1912/13, William Winkworth served as headmaster at St Mary's; (he had previously done so during the spring term of 1898). He was succeeded by Harold Glastonbury, who was appointed headmaster in August 1913, but even his headship was sadly cut short. On the outbreak of war a year later, he enlisted in the army and was killed in action – his wife took over as headmistress at St Mary's and served until 1925. Although the school's next headmaster – Mr G.H. Tolerton – served for five years, success remained elusive.

St Mary's School never had an easy time. Its most successful period had been during the headship of Samuel Vallis junr, under whom there was a 'rapid and sound improvement' – numbers on the roll rose from about 120 to 190 before he moved on. Thereafter the number of pupils fluctuated, rarely exceeding 90 on the roll – a peak of 97 was recorded in 1903 but it dipped to 55 a decade later. In 1912 the school was officially 'warned' for lack of efficiency. After Mr Tolerton took over it improved 'very little if at all' and he resigned in 1930.

In April, 1930, Aubrey Chapman was appointed headmaster of St Mary's School. Things began to

Above: *A group of boys photographed on the field at St Mary's School in about 1950.*
Right: *A group of girls photographed on the field at St Mary's School in about 1950.*

St Mary's School football team 1930/1. Left to right, back row: Mr Chapman (headmaster), J. Wise, W. Goodman, C. Chamberlain; middle row: A. Fowler, W. Vallance, A. Amor; front row: M. Richardson, C. Muttram, A. Blissett, B. Claridge, B. Holland.

Pupils at St Mary's School c.1932. (Left to right, back row: Henry Stacey, John Smith, Cyril Bartholomew, ?, Ray Rogers, Mick Fowler, Charlie Brown, Freddie Dewdney; middle row: Rose Goodman, ?, Sidney McBain, Bobby East, Don Tigwell, Bert Worthy, Win Slade; front row: Peggy Holland, ?, Monica Willis, Flossie Goodyear, Nancy French, ?, ? Muttram.

Pupils of Park Lane School c.1948. Left to right, back row: Bill Spriggs, John Grover, Dave Collins, Dennis Muttram, Geoff Smart, Rodney Gray, George Fuller, Jimmy Collins, Robin Morris; third row: ?, ? Whale, ? Taylor, ? Elliott, ? Blundy, ? Weisman, Denise Taylor, Shirley Rabbetts, Jean Gall, Betty Tanner; second row: Ray Chandler, Andy Tuttle, Bryn Lawrence, Graham Bailey, Bobby Lawes; front row includes: Roy Tubb, Ernie Steer, Gordon Wilkins, David Downes, Mick Smith, Don Stacey, Bernie Hull, Teddy Mann, Cliff Mundy.

The staff at St Mary's School in about 1950. Left to right, back row: Mr Shadlock, Mr Marriott, Mr Colhoon; front row: Mrs Doutre-Hammond, Mr Shaw (headmaster), Mrs Shaw.

St Mary's School cricket team of about 1948. Left to right, back row: Bill Spriggs, Mr Marriott, Andy Tuttle, Rodney Gray, Robin Andrews, Ernie Steer; front row: Douglas Collins, Gordon Wilkins, Robin Morris, John Mann, Richard Down, Ray Chandler, David Down.

change for the better – the much-maligned school garden was soon 'much improved', especially after he obtained plants from Mrs Clarke at the French Gardens. He then set about reorganising the classes at the school to good effect and was able to report that pupils Bernard Brooks and Thomas Goddard had won scholarships to the Newbury Grammar School in 1933. By that same year, the number of pupils on the roll at St Mary's had risen to 135.

However, after the Second World War started and Mr Chapman's wife died, matters began to deteriorate. An inspection in 1943 found the school 'chaotic and unsatisfactory', and a 'statement' was sent to the LEA. When a further inspection later in the year found no improvement, the school managers demanded the headmaster's resignation and Aubrey Chapman readily obliged. With effect from September 1943, the headship of St Mary's passed to Wilfred Shaw. By Christmas, the number of pupils on the roll at the school had increased to 157.

Mr Shaw 'put much untiring labour into the school' and 'did much for the children's happiness' but, from the outset, 'his relations with his staff were not what they should be' it was claimed by Thatcham's vicar, Revd Bernard Thackeray. The two men became embroiled in a dispute about the nature of religious instruction at the school which entered the public domain – even being reported in the local press – and finally brought Mr Shaw's headship at St Mary's School to an end; the managers forced him to resign from his post.

In the spring of 1954, Laurie Turner became the school's headmaster, at a time when Thatcham's village schools were under pressure from the postwar 'baby boom' – St Mary's now had 150 pupils on the roll and more wished to join it but could not be accommodated. To overcome this difficulty, the authorities built a new Church of England school next to the old one. It opened on 20 April 1964. It became St Mary's Junior School, under Mr Turner's headship. (The old school became Dunston Park Infant School, with Mrs Joan Plumridge as headmistress.)

Built to cater for 340 pupils, the new school filled rapidly and – with the addition of temporary buildings – actually accommodated 530 within a few years. The opening of another primary school on a nearby estate in 1972 reduced the number on the roll at St Mary's considerably, and it had fallen to 270 by the date of Laurie Turner's retirement in December 1976. He was succeeded as the school's head by Anne Rowe (by now in charge of a staff of nine full-time teachers) who found that the school was 'very well equipped and very well stocked'.

Over the next quarter of a century, St Mary's School and its neighbour, Dunston Park, continued to be affected by falling numbers. In the new millennium, the authorities felt obliged to take action and it was decided to merge the two schools. Although the schoolmaster's house was sold off in the 1980s the old school remained in use and so a walkway was erected to link it with the new school. Named 'Thatcham Park Primary', and unified under head-teacher Marilyn Cornwell, the school was opened at an official ceremony held on 9 September 2005.

Schooldays at St Mary's School

Memories of schooldays at St Mary's School in Park Lane were recalled by two gentlemen, Mr Dave Cooper and Mr Cecil Hunt, who attended Thatcham's Church of England school before and during the Second World War respectively. It then catered for about 100 pupils aged from 7–14 years – the official school leaving age.

Born in 1925, Dave Cooper lived in Henwick Lane and completed his schooldays at St Mary's, leaving in 1939. The headmaster then was Mr Aubrey Chapman: other teachers included Miss Tryphena Reynolds, who taught the youngest children; Miss West, who cycled in from Bradfield each day; Miss Violet Humphries; and Mrs Freeman, a 'well-built' lady who was given an appropriate nick-name by the pupils! Miss Reynolds and Mrs Freeman had served at the school for many years.

Teaching at St Mary's School in those days had its problems: two classes were taught together in the school hall, separated only by a curtain, so the teachers had to 'talk against one another'. The pupils often deliberately added to the teachers' difficulties – in Mrs Freeman's music lessons, some pupils would disguise their feeble singing with other noises, made by scraping their moveable seats against their desks.

There was plenty of mischief outside the classroom too. The orchard next to the school was a favourite spot for fun and games and its autumn crop provided a plentiful supply of 'ammunition' for 'apple battles'. By all accounts, there was frequent need for recourse to corporal punishment. The cane was administered to the more recalcitrant pupils although its use was not always very effective in curing naughty behaviour.

Scholars at St Mary's Church of England National School line up for a photograph on the school field.

The view looking north up Park Lane in the 1930s towards St Mary's School – Dave Cooper was gardening here one day in 1939 when a runaway barrage balloon floated overhead!

Staff at St Mary's School over half-a-century ago. Left to right, back row: *Fred Shadlock, Bill Marriott (deputy headmaster), Mr Angelo;* front row: *Mrs Doutre-Hammond, Wilfred Shaw (headmaster), Miss Cole.*

Anticipating its use, some pupils would hide the headmaster's cane but the resourceful Mr Chapman was able to create alternative punishments! For example, on one occasion pupil Fred Dewdney was made to hold an iron bar above his head until his arm ached – the whole class felt sorry for him, Dave Cooper recalled.

Being a Church of England school, St Mary's had an annual religious inspection. In one such inspection at this time, Nancy French won the Bishop's Prize whilst Bob Buckle and John Elgar gained certificates. The school was even more proud when its pupils won scholarships to Newbury Grammar School, as Patrick Brooks did in the summer of 1939, for instance.

When war broke out later that summer, Mr Chapman joined the Royal Observer Corps to help protect the village from aerial attack. Opposite the school (where Whitelands Road is today) were the school gardens, so the headmaster's lessons there now offered the pupils an opportunity to do some aircraft spotting. Dave Cooper remembered when an afternoon's gardening was disturbed by a runaway barrage balloon floating overhead – hotly pursued by an aircraft, which finally shot the balloon down at Midgham.

Born in 1932, Cecil Hunt lived in Hollington Place, off Green Lane, and attended the old Infants School in the Broadway before 'automatically' transferring to St Mary's in 1939, the year the war broke out. As a Church of England school, every day started with prayers and on Mondays the vicar, Revd Arthur Owen Daniel, came to the school to give religious instruction. Nuns also came to the school from St Gabriel's Convent at Cold Ash, teaching a class each.

The nuns taught more than just religious education. Cecil Hunt found their lessons more interesting on the whole as they involved creative activities – such as writing a play or making a newspaper – but they taught arithmetic, too, and when they introduced fractions 'that's when they lost me'! Like Dave Cooper, Cecil Hunt enjoyed gardening classes, not least because it was an 'escape from the classroom'.

In 1943 the school got a new headmaster, Mr Wilfred Shaw, but now it was his wife who took the gardening lessons. Unlike Mr Chapman, Mrs Shaw was no aircraft spotter, but Cecil Hunt recalls an occasion during the war when a Spitfire came down on Thatcham Moors and in spite of a police guard on it the local lads managed to get access to it.

This was still a period when boys and girls had separate school playgrounds: at St Mary's the boys had a stone surfaced playground at the front of the school whilst the girls had a tarmac surface on theirs at the rear, beyond which was the 'top field' (now the school playing-field) where games lessons took place. The school toilets left something to be desired in that the boys' urinals were simply walled around – but otherwise open to the elements!

Those pupils who stayed at school for lunch had it delivered by van in containers – lunches were cooked at the Bluecoat School up to 1943 and afterwards at Thatcham's Central Cooking Depot. It was possible to get up to tricks outside lesson times and Cecil Hunt recalls that some pupils would lock one another in the school's boiler house – himself included. More productively, he was in the St Mary's Church choir, under choirmaster Mr Lusty, for which he received 1d. per service – and 1s. for singing at a wedding.

Coming from a sporty family, he made his mark in athletics and has fond memories of school sports days which were held at Crown Meadow in the village: 'We carried down all the equipment required'. Cecil Hunt represented his old school in sport one last time even after he officially left school, at a Thatcham Home Guard fête in the summer of 1946 – he was one of four boys who ran in the St Mary's relay team, for which he received a medal; (the school's girls' team won too)!

A History of the Council School

In the years between the wars, Thatcham's 'new' Council School became an established part of the life of the village. Its first headmaster, Mr H.B. Skillman, retired in 1922 and was succeeded in this post by Mr F.V. Cox B.Sc., LCP. He is remembered as 'a strict disciplinarian' who had 'little time for those pupils who couldn't or wouldn't learn'!

Under his headship, hundreds of local children were educated here between the ages of 5 and 14, then the official school-leaving age. Some of the teachers who had transferred from the old British School continued to serve at the Council School although as the years passed new appointments were made, including that of a new master as assistant headmaster.

By the mid-1920s, new entrants to the school – the youngest infants – were taught by Miss Kate Ashman, before moving on – still as infants – to Miss Minnie Pearce (niece of Rhoda Pearce, who died in 1921). No longer infants, they were afterwards taught by Miss Eleanor Pinnock and then by Miss 'Hettie' Peters – neither of whom suffered fools gladly.

Both of the latter ladies had perfected a technique for dealing with miscreants. It is recalled that 'their practice with an unruly boy was to put him out in the corridor where he would probably be seen by the headmaster and suitably punished'. Next, the older pupils moved on to Mr Reg Taylor (assistant head) and finally to Mr Cox (headmaster) himself.

Mr Cox can be seen in the accompanying photograph with the Council School's Class I (the oldest children) in around 1927. Standing at the back of the classroom with him (third from left) are 'three pupil teachers' – the Misses Stanbrook and Hart, with Arthur Collins – who went on to become full teachers at the school in later years.

As the older teachers retired, pupil-teachers stepped into their shoes, including all three of those in the photograph with Mr Cox. Miss Edna Hart later married Mr Arthur Collins but, sadly, he was killed in action in 1942 (at Singapore during the Second World War). By the late 1920s, the infants were taught by Miss Downton (who became Mrs Ingram).

By the 1930s, Mr Cox had been succeeded as headmaster by Mr Reginald Douglas Lanning, and more new teachers were appointed – one was Miss D. King, daughter of the village hairdresser who had premises in the High Street. Others included Miss Olive Edwards, who joined the school's staff in 1930 and remained a teacher there until retiring in 1972!

Another long-serving Council School teacher was Miss Gwen Lawrence – appointed in 1933, she served there until 1971. A delightful lady, she was another of the school's teachers with an interest in local history and was happy to be interviewed some years ago and recall her memories of what life was like at the school in days gone by.

When she joined the school, there were five classrooms: inside one door were rooms for infants and girls, along with a washing area and cloakrooms; inside another door were three classrooms for the boys, who also had a washing area. The school hall – with a glass partition – was also used as a classroom. The headmaster's room served as the staff room.

'In the girls' and infants' playground there was a small covered area with one long seat' and the lavatories 'were then earth closets', she remembered. 'There was a boiler-room and staff bicycle shed then a boys' playground and school gardens'. In the girls' playground there was a strip of land for a garden and a grass area in which lime trees were planted.

A local farmer lent the school a field nearby – just along the road, on the same side as the school – for boys' football. 'When I first started there, a nurse visited the school regularly,' she recalled, 'and a doctor. Some small children were literally sewn into their clothes'. As the school grew, the British School and Parish Hall were also utilised as classrooms.

Mr Lanning left the school at the end of 1937, and a new headmaster – Mr D.J. Domoney – took up his duties there in the New Year 1938. Douglas 'Jack' Domoney was another Dorset man, born at Stourpaine (near Blandford) who had trained to teach at Winchester College. Aged just 22, he was one of the youngest heads in the country in his first such post.

He came to Thatcham from Riseley, south of Reading, and had not been here long before the outbreak of war brought out his organisational skills coping with an influx of evacuee children who arrived in Thatcham and setting up a school meal service for all the village children at the Bluecoat School in Chapel Street (prior to the opening of the Green Lane Cooking Centre). Gwen Lawrence also recalled this difficult period:

During the war, children from London were evacuated to Thatcham. We taught our own pupils half-days, and the others on the remaining half-days. Later on, some London teachers arrived in the village and taught their children in the British School.

Like the village it served, Thatcham's Council School changed considerably in the postwar years. Mr Domoney remained headmaster for many years to come, but there were staff and other changes in that period. Many of these changes are recorded in notes made by Mr A.E. 'Fred' Shadlock, a teacher from that period, who has supplied much of the information below. Prior to attending training college, he first went to the Council School for a month in the summer of 1947 (the year the leaving age rose from 14 to 15) to observe Miss Gwen Lawrence's lessons.

It was then an 'all-age' school with 489 pupils on the roll. Recalling the school at that time, he says:

Class I (the oldest children) in a classroom at the Council School about 1927. The then headmaster, Mr Cox, is standing at the back (third from left), *with pupil teachers Misses Stanbrook and Hart and Arthur Collins.*

Pupils of Class II at the Council School in 1930 with their teacher Mr Reg Taylor. **Pupils include, back row:** *Doug Durbidge, Roy Joyce;* second row: *Ron Durbidge, Dick Corps, Mary Arnold, Ivy Stacey;* front row: *George Diplock, Lillian Haines, Joan Collins.*

The Council School's football team in 1948 with teachers Mr Laurie Turner (left) and Mr Douglas Domoney (right); players include Les Whincup, Dennis Powers and Alan Owen.

Below: *Council School staff in 1954. Left to right, back row: Miss Lawrence, Mr Graham, Mr Vicarage, Mr Norwood, Mr Malcolm, Mrs Pocock; front row: Miss Hargreaves, Mrs Towers, Mr Domoney (headmaster), Mrs Brown, Mrs Hibberd.*

Funny little things come to mind – the Honours Scholarship Board, a stuffed bird, a picture of The Death of Gelert, *the headmaster's and secretary's office, six classrooms, HORSA blocks then being erected as four temporary classrooms, the woodwork room, the playgrounds and the cycle sheds.*

He particularly remembered the school gardens – gardening was then taken as a school subject, although it is a 'miracle how the rosebushes withstood the trampling of the children's feet'.

He returned to the Council School as a teacher in his own right in the autumn term of 1953. The school's classrooms were then scattered all over the village, 'as the school was bursting at the seams'. The Bluecoat School was then used for domestic science lessons – 'I was highly honoured when invited by senior girls to have lunch with them'. The Conservative Club (next to the New Inn) was used as

a classroom and the Parish Hall was used for medical inspections. The Cadet Hut and the Scout Hut were also being used as classrooms, along with the old British School.

An HMI report on the school that year recounts that the girls 'play netball, coached by the headmaster, and last season they won the senior netball rally of the district'. Football and cricket were played in an adjoining field. PE (or 'drill') was held on the school playground and swimming lessons were held at the Henwick Club pool – a coach took the older pupils there. The annual Newbury Music Festivals were held at the Corn Exchange in March and May – the school entered junior and senior choirs, taken into the town each year by Miss Gwen Lawrence.

Fred Shadlock taught in the British School, which accommodated a class of 40 pupils — they used trestle tables as desks. There were outside toilets and the yard was revived as a playground – 'once a pupil's leg got stuck in the school railings'. Pupils were 'crocodiled' back to the Council School each day for lunch, from 11.55a.m.–1.00p.m. Meals were still brought from the Cooking Depot in Green Lane but Mrs Clarke and Mrs Flack were employed at the school as canteen assistants in 1957 – their duties included serving meals and washing up utensils for return to the depot. 'I have happy memories of teaching at the British School for four years', Fred recalled.

The hall had a large stage with curtains which was ideal for drama. There was no PE equipment so a father donated mattresses. Wet playtimes were no bother as there was plenty of space. The occasional funeral (at the church alongside) necessitated extra quiet lessons and once a drunk squatted outside the school door.

However, pressure on the Council School was alleviated by the building of a new secondary school in the village – the Kennet School – which opened in September 1957.

From this time, the Council School ceased to be 'all-age' and Fred Shadlock returned to teach at its London Road site. The school log book notes that it had:

… assumed a completely different character and is now known as the Thatcham County Primary School. All senior pupils, about 200 in number, have been transferred to the Kennet Secondary School and four teachers have also been transferred.

The staff now consisted of the head and 11 teachers, with 369 pupils on the roll. Later that month, the school was closed for a week because of an 'Asian flu epidemic'.

By 1960, the school was full again and unable to take in further pupils – in April, children aged five

Francis Baily School six-a-side winning football team, 1973, are presented with the cup by Alderman Maurice Paine. Team members were, left to right: Stephen Fleck, David Barr, Graham Hallett, Mike Gabriel (Capt.), Martin Digweed and Graeme Gourlay.

A top junior class (aged 10–11) at work in one of the 'temporary' classrooms at Francis Baily School in 1967.

The top junior boys' football team at Francis Baily School in the mid-1960s – players included Keith Buckle and Martin Lydall.

The top junior girls' netball team at Francis Baily School in the mid-1960s.

Francis Baily School pupils engaged in model making in 1966 following their visit to Hastings to support class work on the famous battle nine centuries earlier.

Francis Baily School pupils engaged in model making in 1969 following their annual school journey to Ludlow to support class work on castles and bridges.

Francis Baily School staff in 1972. Left to right, back row: *Jeanne Jones, Josephine Tucker, Carol Goddard, Rosemary Evans, Philip Panting, Olive Edwards, Ethel Sibley, Mary Lavelle;* front row: *?, ?, Edith Kirk, Terry Dillon, John Martin (deputy headmaster), Fred Shadlock, Gwen Lawrence, Muriel Ingram.*

Francis Baily School staff in 1984. Left to right, back row: *Eileen Hawkins (secretary), Sue Burnell, Fred Shadlock, Vivian Cassell, Peta Collicot;* front row: *Helen Tuck, Gail Hyland, John Green (headmaster), Pauline Moyse, Margaret Hawkins;* seated on grass: *Judy Wright, Jill Smart.*

were 'refused admission' and a further building programme commenced. A new hall, two class-rooms, glass corridor and kitchen were erected by Messrs Cooke Bros, and completed in May 1961. With its own kitchens, a 'cook-in-charge' was now appointed, the first being a Mrs Tench. There were still occasional problems with the older buildings, however – for instance, the toilets froze up and some pipes burst, resulting in a week's enforced closure, in January 1963.

After 25 years, 1960 also saw the retirement of Mr Domoney as headmaster. He was presented with camera equipment to mark the event at a later ceremony, and the Divisional Education Officer commented that his work had always been marked by kindliness:

Even though Thatcham school had been working in difficult, overcrowded conditions during the past ten years, Mr Domoney had shown great patience and had always kept the loyalty of his staff.

Having taught in Berkshire for some 40 years, 'Jack' Domoney died in the Battle Hospital, Reading, on 18 May 1985.

In 1964, under a new head – Mr Edward Helmsley – the village's erstwhile County Primary School was re-named 'Francis Baily School'. A uniform of caps, jerseys and jackets (with a crest) in the school colours, was introduced. From this time, the school's pupils were taken to place flowers on Francis Baily's tomb at St Mary's Church on the anniversary of his birth (28 April) again reflecting a strong interest in local history on the part of some staff at the school. What had once been the village's 'new' school had well and truly come of age!

Schooldays at the Council School

Information about the history of Thatcham is to be found not just in written records but also in the memories of long-time inhabitants of the place. There are still plenty of residents in the town who have recollections of Thatcham in the days when it was a small village and everyone knew everyone. One of them is Mr John Eggleton, who has fond memories of his childhood in Thatcham. He was born at 32 Chapel Street in 1928.

John Eggleton was able to recall his own first day at school, in September 1933. He attended what was then known as the 'Council School' (now Francis Baily School). As a five-year-old, he was taken to school by an older pupil, Miss Ruth Collins, whose family also lived in Chapel Street (being involved with the woodturning firm of Collins & Witts).

In 1933, the Council School had a new headmaster, Mr Reginald Douglas Lanning, who lived close-by at The Laurels in London Road – his daughter, Mary, attended the school and joined the same class as John Eggleton that day. In those days, pupils attended school between the ages of 5 and 14.

At Thatcham's Council School, the pupils started in Class VI (the youngest) and moved up to Class I (the oldest). Mr Eggleton has a photograph of Class VI in 1933: the pupil holding the slate identifying the class is Ivor Halfacree, with John Eggleton immediately to his right. To the left of the picture is the 'class garden' grown from bulbs planted in a wooden tray. Some of the class's artwork can be seen on the classroom walls – the flowers behind the centre dog are labelled 'Tulips' and the poem is 'Little Miss Muffet', complete with a picture of her! There was a school uniform, which – for boys – consisted of green caps, ties and blazers, with TCS (Thatcham Council School) on the outer pocket.

At this date, Class VI was regularly taught by Miss Maskell who lived in a village north of Thatcham. She made an impression on her young charges by travelling to and from school on a motorcycle – quite liberated for the early 1930s! The school day started at 9.00a.m. and finished at 3.30p.m., with an hour for lunch. As there were no school meals at this time, some pupils brought sandwiches but most went home at lunchtime.

As they moved up the school, the pupils were taught by Miss Olive Edwards (Class V), Miss Eleanor Pinnock (Class IV), Miss Gwen Lawrence (Class III), Mr Reg Taylor (Class II) and by the head-master (Class I). Most teachers at that time gave long and loyal service at one school. For example, Miss Edwards joined the Council School aged 18 in 1930, remaining there until 1972; Miss Lawrence gave similar long service here.

In 1934 John Eggleton's family moved to 3 Lower Way, but he remained a pupil at the Council School and has memories of various events from his time there. On one occasion, a teacher sent a boy along to the general store (now a restaurant) in London Road

The view east along Chapel Street towards the Council School – John Eggleton was born at 32 Chapel Street (on the left) in 1928.

Chapel Street, looking east towards Reading, c.1913. The Prancing Horse (right) is no longer a pub.

Pupils of Class VI (the youngest) at the Council School in 1933, with John Eggleton to the right of Ivor Halfacree (holding the slate). The girl (front left) is the headmaster's daughter, Mary Lanning, with Audrey Stanbrook alongside. Other pupils in the photograph include: Ray Collins, Margaret Chilton, Peter Cooper, 'Zebbie' Smith, Chrissie Marshall, Jackie Maggs, Derek Saitch, Jean Giles, Masie Bushell, Chrissie Watts, Jean Breach, George Herbert, Stella Wise, Gloria Goodman, Phillip Panting, John Elgar, Marion Morris, Alfie Haines, Connie Gilmour, Betty Fisher, John Randall, Joyce Chapman and Mabel Hall. Some of them still live in Thatcham.

for 'a tin of elbow grease' as an April Fool's joke. On another, a boy laughed as his teacher read aloud a poem containing the word 'bloody', for which he was caned.

Wednesday, 12 May 1937, was a memorable day for all the pupils at the school, as they celebrated the coronation of King George VI. John Eggleton remembers voting to help elect June Patterson as the school's May Queen and he still possesses his copy of the souvenir coronation booklet – 'The Crowning of the King and Queen'– which Thatcham's Coronation Committee presented to every pupil that day.

The outbreak of war in 1939 affected the school's staffing. Students evacuated from St Charles's College, London, to St Finian's Convent, Cold Ash, filled in as teachers at the school. (John Eggleton still sees one of them, Sister Paddy, around Thatcham today.) He recalls how he and his classmates watched through their classroom window as – across the fields in Station Road – enemy aircraft bombed Thatcham Depot in 1940.

He also remembers 'digging for victory' in the school garden and attending woodwork lessons along at the old Bluecoat School. However, his schooldays finally came to an end when he reached the age of 14 and left Thatcham Council School in the summer of 1942. He has other fond memories of the old village in years gone by.

Pupils at the Council School rehearsing their maypole dance, to be performed at the Broadway green on Coronation Day 1937.

Chapter V

Young Generation, New Generation

Origins of the Kennet School

When the Kennet School first opened its doors nearly half a century ago, it drew its pupils from two dozen villages from an area in the vicinity but also included some villages as far distant as Tadley, Beenham, Hampstead Norris, Brightwalton and Chaddleworth.

The Kennet School admitted its first pupils on 11 September 1957, and was a model for the new schools being built in that period. Construction of the new school had commenced in July 1956, and no expense was spared in its building – indeed, it generated some controversy at the time, with critics claiming that the Kennet School was being built and equipped 'far too extravagantly'. Would it not be better, they asked, to spread the money more widely over the whole district? Others were convinced that it was money well spent.

The Kennet School was built at a cost of £148,000 and originally consisted of a three-storey main block with others adjacent, including the school hall. The critics were confounded when the school – built to accommodate 430 pupils – actually took in over 600 on its first day of operation. The school opened with a staff of 30 teachers under the leadership of headmaster Mr T.G.B. ('Ben') Howe, who came to Thatcham having previously been head of a similar secondary school at Ventnor on the Isle of Wight (staying at the Kennet School until 1960).

Such was the pressure on space at the Kennet School that classes had to use other teaching accommodation nearby, such as the Bluecoat and British Schools, with teachers leading their classes to and from these places each day. 'We send the classes out in rotation', said Mr Howe, 'so that no individual class is put at a disadvantage'. The Kennet School's numbers increased further, so that there were some 720 pupils on the roll in its second year of operation and over 800 in the third. All the while, new classrooms were being built at the Kennet School.

As a secondary modern school, the Kennet School officially catered for pupils aged from 11–15 years (then the minimum leaving age), but the school's policy was to offer all pupils 'of persistence' the opportunity to progress to the limit of their abilities. In the academic year 1958/9, the Kennet School had 24 pupils staying on for a fifth or sixth year and the following year there were around 40 doing so. The school then offered thirteen subjects up to GCE O level standard, including English, maths, history, geography, RE and the sciences.

In keeping with the educational policy of the period, the Kennet School 'streamed' its pupils. Pupils in the A-stream followed a more 'theoretical' curriculum, geared as far as possible to the examining boards' requirements. The B- and C-stream pupils were offered a more practical curriculum and homework for them was left to the discretion of subject teachers. Even greater emphasis on practical work was applied to D- and E-stream pupils, where only 'children with special weaknesses' were encouraged to do homework.

Many of the school's new pupils came from 'older type' rural, all-age schools with more limited facilities. They required a certain amount of readjustment when they began their schooling at the Kennet School. 'They came through this period remarkably

Kennet School's impressive new main block, viewed from Stoney Lane in its early years – it was a model for the schools of the period and critics described it as 'too extravagant'.

Kennet School in the 1960s – here, a PE display is taking place on the field behind the school's main block (where the later lower school building now stands).

well', said Mr Howe. Initially, many were 'diffident' about singing collectively, were not used to changing for PE and had virtually no knowledge of the sciences. 'On the credit side', he added, 'they brought with them an above average knowledge of the 3Rs and habits of study which have since proved invaluable.

The fact that the Kennet School catered for children from a wide locality when it first opened made for some transport difficulties. A fleet of buses conveyed pupils to and from Thatcham at the start and end of the school day but extra-curricular activities were only possible because parents provided car-sharing facilities. Some Thatcham parents even put pupils from outlying villages up in their homes for the night. 'I can't speak too highly of the parents', said headmaster Ben Howe. 'I've taught in secondary schools before, but never have I had the co-operation I receive here'.

For the benefit of children who lived outside Thatcham, the Kennet School duplicated after-school activities during the lunch hour. The range of clubs included chess and photography, country-dancing and canoe-making. The school's facilities included a fully equipped gymnasium and six tennis courts, with sports such as soccer, cricket, rugby, hockey, netball, rounders, athletics and gymnastics on offer. In 1959 there were plans for the school to build its own open-air swimming pool within a year, and by using volunteer labour to keep within a budget of £500. It was finished in July, 1959.

The pool was to be built by members of the school's thriving PTA, which was already holding fund-raising events to fund the project. Their work was further supported by an active governing body, with representatives from the surrounding area, under the chairmanship of Major H. Tracy Barclay. All pulled together to offer the Kennet School pupils the broadest educational opportunities possible, such as careers guidance provided by speakers from the services, industry and other places of interest, along with visits to nearby factories and trips abroad – Paris was the venue in 1959.

The emphasis on practical education then prevalent at the Kennet School was seen in various ways. The school offered a pre-nursing course, for example, and there were eight girls taking advantage of it in 1959. The course gave pupils at least a year over the minimum leaving age (then 15) the chance to become State Registered Nurses, after receiving further training in a hospital. The Kennet School was the only school in the district to have a laboratory specially designed for pre-nursing and biology classes, and its facilities were made available to pupils from other secondary schools in the local area.

A domestic science course provided sound basic training in cookery, laundry and housewifery to girls whose main ambition in life was 'to marry and run a home'. For the boys, furniture-making and canoe-

building were some of the handicrafts on offer in the school's woodwork room. Next door, in the metalwork room, the equipment available included a forge, lathes and a mechanical hacksaw. As an offshoot of work in school's science laboratories, there was a popular science club in which experiments were related to practical matters, such as making a television set and building a radio-controlled aeroplane with a seven-foot wingspan.

The school's art and craft department then taught a range of skills including drawing, painting, linocutting, engraving, typography, modelling and pottery - the school had its own printing machines and pottery wheel. Under the head of art, Mr Fred Stonham, who had exhibited his own work at the Royal Academy, pupils produced limited editions of books, which they illustrated, printed and bound themselves. Such was the standard of art teaching at that date, that every pupil entered by the school for the Royal Drawing Society's examinations succeeded in passing with honours.

The Kennet School's music department had also set itself high standards and made good use of the excellent stage in the school hall, putting on concerts and plays. Under head of music, Mr Wally Brisk, a 60-strong school choir of some quality had been formed and in May 1959, staged a performance of a modern opera – Hugo Cole's *A Statue to the Mayor*. The pupils' interests were further widened by the school's fast growing library, which had been created with stock supplied by the County Library Service but was now being supplemented by gifts from well-wishers.

In 1959 there was more to the Kennet School than all this. The school offered a secretarial course to fifth year pupils, which combined shorthand, book-keeping, typing and office skills and was examined at GCE and Royal Society of Arts standards. In science, there was an incubator where pupils could watch eggs developing into chicks, a wormery, dissecting equipment and easily dismantled models of the human body. A contemporary report in the local press said that a visit to the school at that time was 'in many ways a trip into the educational future' – how true that seems half a century later!

Mr Howe left the Kennet School in December, 1960, going on to become an Inspector of Schools in Worcestershire. His successor was Mr George Hurford, previously head of Icknield School at Wantage; before going there, he had done most of his teaching in his home county of Devon. He came to Thatcham in January 1961 – under his headship, the Kennet School developed in various ways, becoming a community school and acquiring a sixth form.

From being a secondary modern school, it became a comprehensive school in 1971. In December 1972, Prince Philip visited the school – arriving by helicopter – to inspect the work of pupils involved in the Duke of Edinburgh Award Scheme. Mr Hurford

A Kennet School PTA event during the academic year 1965/6: the school's headmaster George Hurford (right) *shakes hands with PTA chairman George Slade* (left).

The staff of the Kennet School are photographed in front of the main block in 1985 – the then headmaster, Dr Nicholas Wheeler-Robinson, is standing at the extreme left.

Kennet School's new sports hall was dedicated to the memory of George Hurford (headmaster 1961–1978) at a ceremony on 3 November 1983 – his wife Mary unveiled a plaque naming it the Hurford Hall.

retired as headmaster in July 1978; returning to his home county of Devon, he lived at Sidmouth, where he died on 20 March 1980, aged 63. He had served the Kennet School well for over 17 years.

In September 1978, Mr Hurford was succeeded as headmaster at the Kennet School by Mr Terence Enright (previously acting head of a Bracknell comprehensive school). He served in this capacity until July 1982, when he was obliged to resign for family reasons; (he went on to become head of a comprehensive school in Sandhurst). The Kennet School's deputy head, Mr Keith Iles stepped into the breach for a term whilst a new appointment was made.

In January 1983, Dr Nicholas Wheeler-Robinson (previously head of Elthorne High School, Ealing) was appointed as head of the Kennet School. He had a local connection, in that he was a nephew of Dr Bradley-Moore, a retired Thatcham GP. After five years, he took early retirement and moved to Pigotts, his family home near High Wycombe, to run his own music activity centre, leaving the school in the charge of acting head Mr Iles for a term again.

In January 1989, Mr Paul Dick took over as headmaster of the Kennet School. He was an ex-head boy of St Malachy's College, Belfast. Having previously been deputy head at Northwood School, Hillingdon, he was just 33 years old when appointed head of the Kennet School and became one of the youngest headteachers in the country. His declared intention was to make the Kennet School 'the best school in West Berkshire' and it was duly included in the 'Good State Schools Guide' for 1993/4, being one of only four Berkshire schools to receive this accolade.

Numbers on the roll at the Kennet School grew steadily under Mr Dick's headship, reaching 1,700 in total by 2006 (with almost 300 in the sixth form). Today the school has distinguished itself by earning 'specialist' status in three subject areas (technology, art and modern languages) and is so popular that it is always oversubscribed when parents in the district choose which local secondary school they wish their children to attend.

Setting up a Village Youth Club

The Kennet School opened in 1957 and in 1961 Mr George Hurford became its second headmaster. He cherished a vision of the Kennet School as a 'community school', with a youth club as a key element. Discussions to open a club at the school were first held in autumn 1962. To this end, a management committee and a members' committee were set up and in January, 1963, the club opened with 30 members, meeting on Friday evenings only at first.

Local man, Mr Horatio 'Ray' Honey, stepped in as the club's first volunteer leader. Well-known in the old village as a keen footballer, he served in the Army during the war and afterwards worked for the Parish Council. He lived at 16 Hartmead Road, near to the school. Under his leadership, plus the loyal support of assistants and an active members' committee, the club quickly established itself and by April had a 'waiting list' of about 50.

Among the assistants were two of the school's staff – PE teacher Ann Sharples and geography teacher Keith Grey – who later married! The club's activities in this period were primarily sporting, such as badminton, trampoline, table tennis, basketball, netball, weight training, rugby, soccer, indoor football, billiards, darts, chess, draughts and – in the summer months – tennis, cricket, archery on pitches in the school playing-fields.

At the club's first 'annual meeting' in October 1963, Mr Hurford – the management committee chairman – spoke proudly about its 'code of conduct'. 'It is our avowed intention to keep standards high', he said, going on to give examples. 'We do not like to see girls in jeans at meetings. We do not permit play on the table tennis courts unless in suitable attire'. A bad habit that was tolerated was smoking – but only 'in the dining space'. How times change!

Given that the club had a waiting list, it adopted strict membership rules. Mr Hurford explained that

A group photo of KYC founder members in October 1963 – Mr Hurford is seated (centre) *with Mr Honey* (to his right).

'members are not allowed to come and go – fines are imposed if attendance is not regular'. In a far-sighted fashion, he told the membership: 'This club is yours. It is going well, and if you go on playing the helpful, active part you have up to the present, I am sure this success will continue'. The future would prove just how right he was!

The school's outdoor pool allowed swimming to be added to the club's summer programme, with other activities – including talks, discussions and films – going on throughout the year. The Duke of Edinburgh Award Scheme was also an important element in the club's activities. By now the youth club had around 160 members and to accommodate them a new youth wing was built at the school – it came into use in the late summer of 1964.

Now known as the 'youth space', a plaque was placed on the wall to record the part which 'Ray' Honey played in getting the club started. It read: 'In recognition of the services of Mr H.H. Honey, Founder Leader of the Kennet Youth Club, Opened 1962'. With effect from 3 August 1964, Mr Honey assumed a new role in his work for Thatcham Parish Council, when he was appointed the local cemetery groundsman.

Mr Honey continued to work voluntarily for the club but from September 1964, a warden (appointed and paid for by the local authority) assumed overall responsibility for the management of its activities. Kennet Youth Club's first such warden was Mr Roy H. Walter. From this time, the club opened on two additional evenings each week, namely Tuesdays and Wednesdays, and the scope of its activities was continually increased.

The club gave support to other organisations, making contributions to the Freedom from Hunger Appeal and to Fair Close Centre for elderly people in Newbury. Assistance was given in the preparation of a playground for physically disabled children at Farley Castle. Club funds were also used to purchase most of what was required for the youth wing – easy chairs, occasional tables plus a range of items of indoor sports equipment.

The new year of 1965 was a high point in the early history of Thatcham's village youth club. The club was run by management and members' committees. The former comprised a dozen or so adults including the school's headmaster, Mr George Hurford (chairman), 'Ray' Honey, Mr Walter (warden), Mr Charlton (county youth officer), Mr 'Bob' Cochrane (parish councillor and school governor), Dr Warwick-Brown (local GP) and Sgt White (local bobby). Mrs Win Flockhart (school secretary) wrote up the committee's minutes.

The other committee comprised about eight members, including David Olley (chairman), Lesley Giles (secretary and treasurer), Janet Burch, Geoffrey Caddy, Linda Hoppe, Donald Hughes, Eileen Peel and Tony Prentice. (The two committees initially met separately, the management committee starting at 7.30p.m. and the members' committee at 8.45p.m. on Monday evenings. The first joint committee meeting was not held until January 1966).

At the management committee meeting held on 11 January 1965, Roy Walter reported that the club's membership then stood at 151. There were 90 boys (28 schoolboys and 90 at work) plus 61 girls (43 schoolgirls and 18 at work). A special event staged at this time was the club's second annual dinner-dance, held on Saturday 23 January. A sub-committee was set up to arrange it and decided that members attending from 7.00p.m. (to take part in the dinner) would be charged 7s.6d. but those wishing to attend the dance only (from 9.00p.m.) should pay just 3s.

A number of local worthies were invited along as guests – including the wives and husbands of management committee members – and the dinner tables were set out in the shape of an E, with reserved seating for those at the top table. A non-alcoholic punch was concocted for club members beforehand and toasts – for the Queen, the club, the visitors and appropriate replies – were made with 'fruit cup'. The dance was deemed 'successful'.

Also successful that New Year was the club's netball team, coached by Mrs Betty Slade. The KYC team won their area final at St Bart's School on January 17, beating Theale YC 22–1. They went forward as area champions to represent South Berkshire in the county tournament at Little Heath School, Tilehurst, on 30 January. The KYC girls battled their way through the rounds and beat Wantage YC in the final to become County Champions.

Then, on Wednesday 24 February came KYC's official opening ceremony, conducted by Sir John Hunt CBE DSO DCL LLB, leader of the first ascent of Mount Everest in 1953 and Director of the Duke of Edinburgh's Award Scheme by 1965. The VIPs at the event included Sir George Mowbray (County Council Chairman), Mr T.D. Whitfield (Director of Education), Mrs Adams (County Youth Section Chairman) and other officials.

In a topical speech, Sir John Hunt declared that opening a new youth centre was far more exciting than the launching of a space satellite. 'Many projectiles were orbiting the Earth for the express purpose of demonstrating a country's superior technology and way of life', he said; but the launching of a youth centre was a much more important event, enabling people 'to get know each other, helping them to live in harmony on this planet'.

Following its official opening in February 1965, the village youth club went on to establish itself as a permanent fixture in Thatcham. It was obliged to change with the times, of course, but that ensured its survival. The 1960s was a liberated decade and no institution could afford to ignore this fact. Kennet Youth Club was no exception and even in its formative period changes occurred in both its management and its programme.

Its early strict regime was gradually eased and the job title of the person in charge on a day-to-day basis was changed from the slightly off-putting 'warden' to 'youth leader'. These appointments coincided with academic years and the post-holders also taught at the Kennet School. The first post-holder was Roy Walter, who taught in the school's PE Department, no doubt a reflection his own enthusiasm for sport.

Not surprisingly, he arranged fixtures between club and school teams. For boys, football and rugby were

Some of the founder members of KYC, c.1964. Left to right, back row: *Denny Banner, Dave Wise, Fred Lewis, Eric Panting, John Ives and Derek Chivers;* front row: *Helen Rament, Carol Brown, Lesley Giles, Andre Honey (daughter of Mr Ray Honey).*

both popular: 'We played a rugby match against the School which resulted in a draw', he reported in January 1965. The girls' sport was netball: 'Two netball matches have been played, one against the School which we lost and one against another local club which the Kennet Youth Club won', he reported at the same date.

Roy Walter had been assisted by two Kennet teachers – Ann Sharples and Keith Grey (who later married) – who helped with the sporting activities, but the pair moved on at the end of the autumn term in 1964. However, 'Ray' Honey remained a loyal helper to the club, organising social activities such as dances with the support of ladies like Mrs Rayment, Mrs Thompson and Mrs Mills, 'our most capable ladies behind the counter'.

This was a reference to the club's coffee bar – a popular facility with members. An extension to it was built during 1965 and extra stools were purchased. However, there were concerns at this time that KYC catered more for boys than girls as 'many' of the latter were 'losing interest in the club and leaving'. As a solution, Roy Walter stated that he 'would like to arrange some lectures on make-up and hair styling for the girls'.

Another bone of contention was the club's Duke of Edinburgh Award Scheme. Pursuits included first aid, shooting, horsemanship, gymnastics, trampoline, chess, and table tennis – but initially only for boys! Plans to extend the scheme to girls were discussed at KYC's first joint management and members' committee meeting in January, 1966. Later, a course of first-aid lectures was accepted as the girls' first step in entry to the scheme.

At the start of 1965, Roy Walter also suggested introducing 'an annual club walk' each April. In the event, all the district's youngsters competed in an annual walk each May, between Newbury and Andover, starting from each town in alternate years – the 1966 event was 'the wettest-ever'. KYC members always did well in this event – its boys' team won at least once and its girls' (or 'ladies') team was first over the line at least twice.

In March, 1966, KYC boys' football team beat 15 others in the area final, going on to represent South Berkshire in the county final of the indoor contest at Arborfield. Here, they got through to the semi-final but were beaten by eventual winners, Edgebarrow. At Easter, Roy Walter led six KYC boys on a camping and canoeing course on the Kennet but he was nearing the end of his time as club leader, moving on in the summer of 1966.

In September 1966, he was succeeded as KYC youth leader by Neil Warnock, a Liverpudlian who had trained at Culham College. Under him, club members first used the new floodlighting system on the school's outdoor courts, which allowed games to be played after dark. He stayed for two years but in September 1968, set off with three friends to make his

Left: *The KYC Netball team who won the championship in two consecutive years, 1965/1966. Left to right, back row: Maureen Holbon, Mrs Betty Slade (coach), Veronica Holland, Pauline Joyce; front row: Bridget Eaton, Marilyn Sowden, Georgina Slade, Maureen Pearce.*

Right: *Dick Partridge, KYC leader from 1968–1987.*

Far right: *John Stopps, temporary KYC leader 1975/76.*

Kennet Youth Club 'ladies' set out on the district's annual Newbury–Andover walk, c.1966. Left to right: Susan Burton, Cynthia Walters, Georgina Slade, Marilyn Sowden, Janet Thorne, Jane Blanchard.

way to Australia. He arrived in time for Christmas and now lives there.

In September 1968, Dick Partridge became the next leader of KYC and stayed until 1987. In his years as leader, KYC membership grew to nearly 500. He organised the successful reunion of old members in February 1985, at which one of those present was Mrs June Cockerill – who still had the first membership card issued when the club opened in January 1963. Since its foundation over 20 years earlier, the Kennet Youth Club had come of age! Another two decades later – in September 2004 – the club moved into purpose built premises on one of the town's new estates and was renamed the Moorside Youth Club.

The Early Years of Parsons Down School

Some of the first intake of pupils at the new Parsons Down School enjoying the play equipment in September 1972.

Forty years ago, when the town's population was growing fast, there was a shortage of primary school places in Thatcham. It was made more acute by the closure of two old village schools – St Mary's School in the Broadway and St Barnabas School at Crookham. So plans were made to open two new schools on Thatcham's burgeoning estates – Whitelands and Parsons Down Schools.

Parsons Down School was built on the edge of what was then a new estate centred on Paynesdown Road. The whole estate occupied a greenfield site on one of Thatcham's old medieval open fields –

A top class (aged 10–11) at Parsons Down Junior School in 1986.

The staff of Parsons Down Primary School in 1975. Left to right, back row: Annette MacWilliam, Margaret Richardson, Ann Allen, Jenny Franey, Robert Wellman, Gill Underwood, Pauline Williams, Janice Schofield (currently headteacher of the Infant School); front row: Sue Plackett, Graham Stephens, Geoff Davies, Anne Murray, Ellie Holland.

The staff of Parsons Down Junior School in 1986. Left to right, back row: *Brenda Harland, Wynne Frankum, Ann Allen, David Strauss, Christine England, Val Boniface, Sue Plackett;* front row: *Andrew Allport, Pam King, Rob Ashmore, Sheila Hunt, Alan O'Caine.*

Parsons Down Infant School's 1986 Christmas production – the pantomime Dick Whittington.

'Le Personnesdoune', or 'Painsdown' Field as it had become by the nineteenth century. This was land that was owned by the church in the middle ages but between 1967 and 1971 the Paynesdown Road estate – comprising some 326 houses – was built by Messrs Wimpey Ltd, and a new school was needed.

The school was intended to open at Easter 1972, but construction work overran. However, the school was finished that summer so the school opened a term late on Tuesday 5 September. The building had been designed to accommodate 280 children. The pupils were admitted by year group over several days so that there were only 10 pupils in school that first day, but eventually there were 180 pupils aged from five to eleven. The school's teaching staff consisted of a 'teaching head' and five further teachers.

Parsons Down's first headteacher was Mr Geoffrey Davies LCP, who came here having previously been head of Harwell Primary School in Oxfordshire. He designed the school's badge, depicting a lion in charge of the arms of the Mount family of Wasing Place, the last lords of the manor of Thatcham. The 'jagged mound' on which the lion stands came from the arms of the Croft family, who owned the manor of Thatcham in the eighteenth century. The 'Mount' lion was actually blue but it was changed to red on the badge.

This reflected the fact that Mr Davies was a native of Wales – by incorporating the colours red, silver and green into the school badge, it now depicted his national colours! He shared the teaching of the school's junior pupils with teachers Mrs Ann Stania and Mrs Sue Plackett; the infants were taught by Mrs Dawn Saunders, Miss Ann Jones (who later became Mrs Murray) and Miss Ellie Stewart (who became Mrs Holland when she married on 2 December 1972). Mrs Marjorie Trapp was the school's welfare assistant.

Ancillary staff at the school from that date included Mrs Wendy Rumble (secretary), Mrs Vera Wane (cook) and Mr Reg Scaplehorn (caretaker). Further teaching appointments were made as the academic year progressed, including that of a deputy head-teacher from March 1973. (At the start of the following academic year, Mr Graham Stephens was appointed as the deputy head). A school association

(PTA) was established, with headteacher Mr Davies as its president and Mr Michael Ansley, a parent, as its first secretary.

Parsons Down School's first year was a busy one. The Berkshire String Players gave a concert at the school in October; there was a visit to the Science Museum in March; and a trip to South Wales in June. The school's fund-raising committee raised £30.67p at a jumble sale in February, £60.46p at a mini-market in March and £84.45p at a grand fête in May. A spring dance was held in March and a barbecue dance in June. Sports day took place on July 4 and the school's first academic year ended successfully on Friday 20 July 1973.

The school's open-plan design came in for some criticism, although it was a feature of the times. Mr Davies defended it, and the fact that pupils were allowed to leave their desks to talk to each other or to their teacher. 'Far more is learnt from discussion than by sterile application to text books, to the exclusion of all else', he said. 'In fact, forcing children to sit still for long periods, without permitting any conversation, borders on physical cruelty'. If the need arose, the school 'did have some punishment', he added.

Parsons Down School soon became over-subscribed and six years after the original school opened a new junior school was built off Herons Way. That opened in January 1979, whereupon the original school became an infant school only – it opened as such on 9 January under head teacher Mrs Jan Malsingh. Mr Davies transferred to the new junior school – together, the schools now had 427 pupils. The junior school continued to grow but, aged 61, Mr Davies retired as head teacher at the end of the summer term, 1986.

Mr Rob Ashmore, who had previously taught at British Forces' schools in Germany, succeeded him as head of Parsons Down Junior School. It was under his headship that the National Curriculum was implemented, with computer technology being an integral part of the children's education. He was obliged to step down through ill health and eventually took early retirement in December 2003. Miss Julie Moore, the school's deputy head, served as acting head until Mrs Petrina Winsor was appointed as headteacher of the school from September 2004.

Chapter VI
People and Places: Part One

In Memory of a Thatcham Hero

Right at the end of Queen Victoria's long reign, the Boer War (1899–1902) broke out. Before it was over no fewer than 90 of the young men of Thatcham had volunteered to serve in South Africa. Four of them never came back. Messrs Haines, Hawkins, Munday and Peirce – the latter the son of Thatcham's vicar at that time – were killed in the fighting.

However, another young man from Thatcham – William House – not only came back from the war but also brought back with him the coveted Victoria Cross. He was born in 1879, the eldest son of Thomas and Sarah House of Park Lane. He had been a Bluecoat boy before he joined the Army at the age of 17. He went to South Africa with the 2nd Battalion of the Berkshire Regiment on 12 February 1898.

Private House performed an act of 'conspicuous bravery' on 2 August 1900. In the face of heavy enemy fire at Motsilikatse Nek, a mountain pass west of Pretoria, he broke cover and dashed to the rescue of a wounded sergeant. After carrying Sergeant Gibbs a short distance, House was hit in the head by two Mauser bullets; although badly injured, he called out to his comrades not to come to his rescue as the enemy fire was so severe.

For his gallant action, House was awarded the DCM in 1901 but the following year this was cancelled and the VC was conferred on him instead. House returned to Thatcham a hero and visited his mother, then widowed and living in Chapel Street in July 1902. He stayed on in the army and was promoted to lance corporal in the First Royal Berkshire Regiment.

Tragically – perhaps as a result of his head wounds – William House committed suicide at Shaft Barracks, Dover, on 27 February 1912, at the age of 32. He was buried in an unmarked grave in St James' Cemetery, Dover. In recent times, his regiment has amalgamated with others to become the Royal Gloucestershire Berkshire and Wiltshire Regiment.

William House's achievement was belatedly recognised on 21 July 1994, when a tombstone inscribed '... in memory of a courageous soldier' was placed on his grave by his regiment at a special ceremony held before a large audience. His Victoria Cross is now held in the small regimental museum at Brock Barracks, Reading. In Thatcham, William Close – a road on a modern estate – is named after him.

Interestingly, Thatcham has produced not one but three Victoria Cross winners, the other two being brothers and the sons of Major Charles Turner of Thatcham House. He had himself served with the

The first of three Thatcham men to win the VC – Pte William House of the 2nd Battalion, Berkshire Regiment, who was awarded the medal for his brave action in the Boer War.

Chapel Street looking east in the early years of the twentieth century – William House's widowed mother was living here in 1902 when he returned to the village as a Boer War hero.

Thatcham Broadway c.1930 – the War Memorial carries the names of men from the village who were killed in action; William House's achievement was belatedly commemorated in 1994.

Berkshire Regiment from 1881 until 1902 and his second wife was Jane Elizabeth Buller, herself a descendant of a famous Boer War general.

One of their sons – Alexander Buller-Turner – died on 1 October 1915, after being wounded in an attack on a German position; he was buried in the military cemetery at Choque, France. With his men, another son – Victor Buller-Turner – captured an enemy position in Egypt's Western Desert on 27 October 1942, and lived to tell the tale. Both were awarded the VC.

Memories of Village Traders

A quarter of a century ago, an ex-resident of Thatcham was kind enough to recall his younger days in the village. His family had lived at Harts Hill since the early part of the nineteenth century. He was the late Mr George Stocker, who had been born in the parish in 1909 and spent the first 50 years of his life here, and whose memories went back to the 1920s. Mr Stocker was able to remember many of the tradesmen who had businesses in the village in those days and he did so in the form of a journey through Thatcham's main streets, starting near the old Council School. Travelling westwards past Stoney Lane and the Plough Inn, the first shop he recalled was 'Benny's', in the front room of a row of terraced cottages.

This 'wee sweetshop' was kept by Mrs 'Benny' Franklin and was regarded as the tuck shop by pupils at the nearby school.

It was well patronised by the children for the spending of their pennies and ha'pennies – aniseed balls, mint humbugs and sherbet bags were favourite purchases.

Opposite Mrs Franklin's shop was a large horse pond, known to local children as 'Benny's Pond'. In the winter, when frozen over, it was much used for sliding. It became redundant as a horse pond and was filled in during the 1930s. Further along Chapel Street was a baker's shop (No.76) owned by Mr Frederick Rosier, and later by Mr A. J. Pearce.

Almost opposite Turnfields was a blacksmith's shop (No.64). Mr Stocker remembered:

Its genial owner and smith was George Pike, who seemed content to suffer a frequent audience of small boys. They leaned over the smithy's half-door to watch while new shoes were fitted to horses ranging from ponies to carthorses.

Close by was a grocer's shop, owned by Mr Jim Matthews, and also two smaller shops. One of these was a sweetshop (No.34) run by Mrs Billy Nightingale and the other was a greengrocer's store

owned by Mr Tommy Rodgers. 'He was a bewhiskered and rather irascible old chap' who often complained, with just cause, about 'dratted boys' stealing from his allotment!

The Broadway was the focal point of the village. Immediately before its junction with Chapel Street there was a saddler's shop and a shoe shop, both belonging to Messrs S. and F. Ashman. Further along – 'and sadly since vanished' – were the premises of the following traders: James Pike (outfitters), David Collings (ironmongers) and C.G. Brown (clock repairer).

Continuing westwards into the High Street, on the north side was the corn merchant's shop (No.3) kept by Mr Bernard James Brooks & Sons. This was followed by Lay's, the grocers (Nos 5–7), staffed by the two brothers Bill and Bert Lay and their ever-cheerful lady assistant Miss Jenny Pike. The shop traded under the slogan 'It pays to shop at Lays'.

'This was the shop where my parents procured most of their groceries, and what a pleasure it was to be sent there on some mission', recalled Mr Stocker. This was long before the modern era of supermarket shopping. 'In those days customers were received with courtesy, their needs met from nests of drawers and individually wrapped – quite unlike today!'.

Next to Lay's shop was another grocer's shop owned by Mr Tom Cousens. 'He was a delightful character', remembered Mr Stocker, 'possessing a great sense of humour'. At the side of his shop was an alleyway leading off the street to a row of cottages. This alley was known in the old days as 'Soapsuds Alley' because of the soapsuds, which flowed down it into the gutter, on washdays.

A little further on was the ladies' and gents' outfitters shop of Mr Alfred Gibbs & Son, and then the sweetshop and florists (No.29) kept by Mrs Randall. Over on the south side of the High Street was the ironmongery (No.32) of Mr F. J. Reynolds. It was later kept by Mr Charles Pazzard, who also traded as a furniture, china and glass dealer and hardware merchant.

Next came Church Lane, beyond which was the confectionery shop (No.33) run by Mrs Adams. 'Her husband, Charlie, another genial character, was bakery roundsman for the Lay brothers', recalled Mr Stocker. They ran a bakery business as well as their grocery. 'In those days bread was baked in wood fired ovens and was absolutely delicious'. Mr Adams delivered bread to Harts Hill and Bucklebury.

'He was always ready to play cricket with us boys if we had a game in progress'. In fact, 'most of the village traders were kind and friendly people in those days', concluded Mr Stocker. Most knew the village children by their Christian names and addressed them as such if they behaved themselves – as the good book says, 'these were merciful men whose righteousness hath not been forgotten'.

Above: *St Mary's Church in about 1910 – as it would have been in George Stocker's childhood days. The photograph was taken from a field in which houses have been built today.*

Right: *The view up Harts Hill Road towards Bucklebury in 1904. On the left is the entrance to Harts Hill Farm.*

The Broadway looking north towards Chapel Street in about 1908 – the tradesman's vehicle is one of many that plied the village streets when George Stocker was a boy.

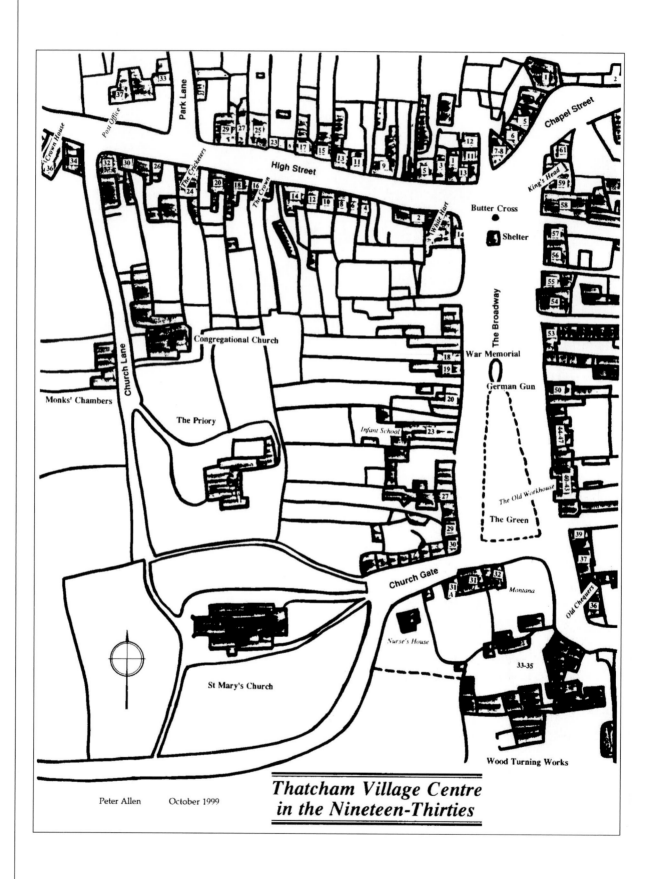

Thatcham Village Centre in the Nineteen-Thirties

Peter Allen   October 1999

Thatcham in the 1930s

Thatcham is a parish intersected by the river Kennet and the Kennet and Avon canal, with a station 1 mile southeast from the village, on the Great Western Railway. The village is lighted with gas and electricity, and is supplied with water by the borough of Newbury. The living is a vicarage, net yearly value £400, with residence, and 11 acres of glebe, in the gift of Lancing College, and held since 1932 by the Revd Arthur Owen Daniel MA of Selwyn College, Cambridge. The soil is gravel and clay; subsoil, gravel, clay and peat. The chief crops are barley, wheat and roots. The area of the civil parish is 5,575 acres of land, including the commons & c.

KEY:

The Broadway:

1: Thatcham Road Transport Services, TN 22–23. 5: William Hall, barber and hairdresser. 7–8: Robert Wyatt, butcher and dairyman; (by 1935 the business was kept by Lionel Baker, TN 41). 11: Charles G. Brown, jeweller and watch-repairer. 12: Martin & Son, pork butcher; (the business was previously kept by Sidney Goldfinch). 13: Mrs H. 'Rosie' Holloway, confectionery and cakes. 14: Henry George Couzens. 18: Albert Edward Phillips, bakery at rear of premises. 19: Ernest John Rufey, groceries, sweets and tobacco. 20: Percy Bradley, shoe-shop; (previously Frederick George Spanswick, carrier and bus proprietor). 23: Church of England Infant School (headmistress Miss Blanche Green of 14 Bath Road, Thatcham). 27: Thomas Maccabee, carpenter. 29: Mr M. Green, on lease from Crookham estate. 30: Mr C. Hutchins, on lease from Crookham estate. 31: Mr William Butler, private residence. 32: George Leslie Barker, wireless dealer, TN30. 33: John Brown & Sons, woodturning works, TN12. 36: Frederick Job Chandler, beer retailer. 37: George Wheeler, blacksmith etc. 39: Mr and Mrs H. Hunt (Hunt's kinsman's almshouse). 44: Mrs Farr. 45: Mrs Smith. 46: Mrs Gray. 47: Mrs Giles (all Hunt's Charity Amshouses for the poor). 50: Edmund Pinnock, coalmerchant etc. 53: David Collings, hardware, stationery, toys, etc. 54: Charles Whitehouse, clock and watch repairs. 56: John Henry Pike, draper and outfitters. 57: Wilfred Fuller, newsagent. 58: Charles George Brown junr, coach and van works. 59: Ernest H. Hawkins, beer retailer.

The High Street: *1: Thomas James Oakley, chemist and druggist. 3: Bernard James Brooks, corn merchant, TN40. 5: Alfred Edward Mooring, grocer, wine merchant. 9: Westminster Bank Ltd. Open Tuesdays/Fridays. 13: Lloyds Bank Ltd. Open Tuesdays/Fridays. 15: Mr Henry Robbins, private residence; previously Bartholomew 'Barty' Fulbrook, barber. 17: Robert Gordon Byng, grocer. 23: Mr Henry James Brown, parish sexton. 25: Alfred Gibbs, ladies and gents outfitters. 27: Thomas King, hairdresser. 29: Mrs Elizabeth Randall, sweets and tobacco. 33: Charles Bevan, chemist and druggist. 35: Basil Edgar Gilmour, post office and tobacco. 37: Edward John Mecey & Son, solicitors. 2: John Williams, beer retailer. 4: Arthur William Mason, cooked meat shop. 6: Mr John W. Wheeler, private residence. 8: Mr Isaac Lewis, private residence. 10: Mr A.B. Bland, Relieving Officer, No. 2 District. 12: Anthony P.J. Stacchini, printer, Thatcham Press. 14: William Golding Lay & Sons, grocer. 16: George and Amy King, beer retailers. 18: Mrs I.M. Styles, circulating library. 20: Mr Thomas Headlong, private residence. 24: Ernest Welch, beer retailer. 26: Gilbert Henry Buckell, boot and shoe maker. 30: Mr Albert Smith (head gardener at Thatcham House), private residence. 32: Charles Pazzard, ironmonger and hardware dealer. 34: Mrs Maud Adams, refreshment rooms, grocers and provision merchants, TN 90. 36: Thomas George Gandy, wheelwright. 2 Chapel St: Mrs Emma Woodbridge, dairy farmer. 61: Frank Ashman, boot repairer.*

A Thatcham Childhood

An old Thatcham resident interviewed a quarter of a century ago was Mrs Aleithia Carnell. She was born in London but came to the village at the age of three, in 1907. She enjoyed a Thatcham childhood, therefore, at a time when the population of the place was only a little over 2,000 people. Her family lived at No.48 The Broadway (now part of the Kingsland Centre), the home of her grandmother, Mrs Eliza Headlong.

The Headlongs were a long-established Thatcham family with several branches. A cousin, Arthur Headlong, was well-known in the village as 'Dutch' and delivered coal for Pinnocks, the Broadway coal merchants. When he died, his coffin was transported to the cemetery in London Road on the back of one of the firm's lorries.

Pinnocks were also 'carriers' to the GWR and Mrs Carnell remembered Frank Pinnock, who plied to and from Thatcham railway station. Sometimes he drove a horse-drawn wagonette, other times a pony and trap. Passengers paid 6d. each way for the ride but, if Mr Pinnock was in the right mood, the local children would often be able to hitch a ride free.

Other childhood memories are of Sunday afternoon picnics on Thatcham Moors, a favourite with village families then. Across the railway line there was a clear spring and a shallow stream where children could paddle. Sunday school outings were even more of a treat: one of Farmer Woodbridge's wagons was used to convey the children up to Crookham Common.

As they left the village, the children waved flags and their parents saw them off. At the bottom of Crookham Hill everyone got off the wagon and walked to the top – this was to spare the horses! Up on the common, there were games and races, followed by tea in a barn, and then home to bed.

Schooldays for Mrs Carnell were spent at the British School in Church Lane. When this school closed in 1913, the children and their teachers transferred to the new Council School (now Francis Baily). She remembered especially Mr Skillman, Miss Pearce and Miss Pinnock.

Before the First World War 'votes for women' was a major issue and Thatcham played a part in the campaigns of the time. Mrs Carnell recalled seeing meetings on the Broadway green where local women – such as Mrs Munro Ashman and Mrs Grace Fuller – made speeches alongside suffragettes who had travelled down from London, the celebrated Mrs Pankhurst among them. In a place like Thatcham, their reception was mixed: men from Colthrop Mill came along to heckle and throw fruit at the speakers during their lunch-hour.

Less controversially, Mrs Carnell recalled the days when horses stopped to drink from the horse-trough at the Tomlin fountain in the Broadway and how the old men of the village sat in the shelter, smoking their pipes and 'gossiping'. One character who regularly sat on the seat in the Broadway was Charlie Bradbury. He lived at Thatcham Newtown (St John's Road): being a cripple, he hobbled along to the village centre on crutches, only to be teased by the local lads.

Of local traders, John Pike the draper brought back fond memories. From his shop in the Broadway he sold shoes and 'button boots' and allowed his customers to take a few pairs away in a bag. They were able to try them on in the comfort of their own homes and choose the best fit, returning the rest to the shop. 'It would never happen today', thought Mrs Carnell.

Elsewhere in the Broadway was the grocery and sweetshop then kept by Mr and Mrs Walter Holdup, and later by their daughters Gladys and Vera (No.19). Round in the High Street was the sweet shop (latterly a tyre depot) run by Mrs Randall, a favourite with village children. An ice-cream cornet – with homemade ice-cream – could be had for a ha'penny, and 1d. would buy four 'everlasting strips' or 12 aniseed balls.

The premises of Messrs Pinnock, the Broadway coal merchants and carriers – Frank Pinnock is seen here with his wife and son, and Arthur Headlong who delivered coal around the village.

The Tomlin memorial at the top of the Broadway around the time of the First World War – the motorcycle and engineering works of Messrs Brown can be seen (right) next to the King's Head.

Growing Up in Old Thatcham

Mark Browning, the rag-and-bone man from Thatcham Newtown, with his horse and cart – from these humble beginnings he rose to become 'a man of property'.

Some years ago, memories of life in the old village of Thatcham were recalled by Mrs Margery Roper, who then lived in Barfield Road. She came to Thatcham in 1914, at the age of four, to live in Chapel Street with her grandfather, chimney sweep George Lake.

Her earliest memories of the village were shaped by the seasons: playing in Stoney Lane and Harts Hill roads before they were tarmacked, for instance. In summer, the streets were dry and dusty but in winter they were quite the opposite.

In summer the inhabitants of the parish walked down to the canal where there were several favourite spots for swimming. In winter they found places to skate and slide, such as the pond – now filled in – on The Marsh (Dunstan Green), or the old gravel pit in Lower Way. In exceptionally cold winters even the canal froze over and tempted many skaters – but immersions took place when the ice gave way!

On special occasions there was the local custom of 'anvil-firing' to make celebrations go with a bang! The earliest that Mrs Roper could recall was for the Armistice in November, 1918. Coronations and jubilees were also marked by anvil-firing: the anvils would be set up in the Broadway and Freddie Davies would emerge from the smithy in Brown's yard with a red hot poker to fire them – sadly this custom is no longer allowed.

Like most village children, Mrs Roper was sent on errands, for example to fetch fuel for heating and cooking. The woodturning works at the bottom of the Broadway supplied woodchips, at 2d. a sack, which were useful for lighting open fires. Other offcuts – such as 'ends' cut from brushstocks – could be purchased by the bushel. Families with the (then) more modern closed cooking ranges would buy bags of coke from Mr Corderoy at the gas works in Station Road.

Growing up, there were other distractions for young people in Thatcham 80 years ago. Mr Mayow, a local railwayman, organised dances at the Parish Hall. Popular dances then were the 'Lancers' and quadrilles.

More of a novelty were the silent movies arranged by Mr Stacchini, the High Street printer. There were Saturday afternoon and evening showings, at which Dolly Hamblin played the music for silent films featuring stars of the time, such as Tom Mix and Pearl White. On winter evenings, some local people made their own entertainment in the village amateur dramatics group. One of its members then was Mrs Alice Topley, wife of the High Street butcher Mr Archibald Topley.

In summer, there were trips to the seaside – usually Southsea – in Mr Durnford's charabanc. With solid tyres and bench seats the journey, which must have taken a couple of hours, was quite an experience, but everyone enjoyed themselves. The earliest trip Mrs

Mobile traders sold their wares in Thatcham's streets at that time. On Saturdays, Mr Eighteen the fishman came from Reading with a horse and cart from which he sold herrings and bloaters at 1d. each. Tommy Pratt traded as a rag-and-bone man in the same fashion – he and his wife were a familiar sight in the village streets with their donkey cart. Mrs Pratt was dumb but this didn't stop her from beating poor old Tommy with a stick as well as their donkey!

Mark Browning, of Thatcham Newtown, also traded as a rag-and-bone man. Children would exchange jam jars for windmills or rabbit skins for cash – Mrs Carnell remembers that they fetched 2d. a time. Mark Browning's story is one of true entrepreneurial enterprise: he went to work at Colthrop Mill but was sacked by John Henry, the proprietor, for some misdemeanour. As a family man, he sorely missed the 11s. a week the job paid.

However, Mark set up on his own as a rag-and-bone man and managed to scrape a living. Trade grew and he was able to buy himself a horse and van, allowing him to collect waste paper to sell to the very mill from which he had been sacked! He went on to become a 'marine dealer and storesman' – of some repute locally – and also a 'man of property', as he bought the block of buildings which included the house in which he and his family lived.

The view north into Thatcham Broadway around the time of the First World War. Anvil firing took place on the green – the earliest Mrs Roper recalled was for the Armistice in 1918.

The thatched cottages in Chapel Street around 1914 – in that year, at four years of age, Marjorie Roper came to live in the street with her grandfather George Lake.

The view west along Chapel Street about 1930 – Mrs Roper witnessed the disastrous fire at Collins & Witts woodturnery works behind the Parish Hall (left distance) around this time.

Roper remembered was to the Wembley Exhibition in 1922.

Everyday life in Thatcham at that time was slower but by no means dull. Living in Chapel Street, Mrs Roper was one of the first people in the village to witness the disastrous fire, which engulfed Messrs Collins & Witts woodturnery works in 1932. Their yard was located behind the Parish Hall: at about 2.00a.m. one morning, a fire took hold and burned the premises to the ground, attracting a large crowd of villagers from their beds.

Most of the time, of course, local businessmen carried on their trade without hindrance. In Chapel Street, Mrs Roper remembered traders like Tommy Rogers, who kept a greengrocery. Then there was Mrs Hanson, who sold sweets and cigarettes from her front room and hired out bicycles at 3d. an hour. Close by, Fred Joyce ran a little shop known to the villagers as the 'dinky stores'.

Also in Chapel Street were the premises of Tom Maccabee, the village undertaker. In a shed beside his house he plied his trade – making coffins was all part of his service!

Around the corner, in the Broadway, even more of the commercial life of the village was carried on. Edmund Pinnock sold coal from his yard here and plied daily to and from Thatcham railway station in his 'cab'. Next door, David Collings' shop sold hardware and a miscellany of other goods.

At the bottom of the Broadway, Fred Chandler kept the Old Chequers pub with his daughter Lottie, whilst at the top end Martin & Son traded as pork butchers – the son was Cecil, who drove their delivery van around the neighbourhood. No wonder many elderly inhabitants remember old Thatcham as a cosier place than the busy town it has become today.

When Everyone Knew Everyone

Many elderly residents of Thatcham are people who look back fondly to a time when everyone knew everyone else in the old village. Two of them who were interviewed some years ago were brother and sister Mr Joe Mace and Mrs Olive 'Ivy' McJohnston (née Mace). Joe was born in 1909 and Ivy was ten years his junior – their parents were Mr William 'Billy' Mace and his wife Alice.

The family home was then a cottage in the row (demolished in 1958) where Elms Avenue, on the south side of Chapel Street, is today. 'It was a smashing place when we were kids', Joe and Ivy agreed. 'We used to play with spinning tops in the road and roll our hoops – hardly any motor traffic came through in those days'.

As children, Joe and Ivy recalled how sheep and cattle were driven through the streets of Thatcham 'on the hoof' en route to Newbury market. Much more exciting was the annual visit to Newbury of George Sanger's circus, when the animal cages were trundled along the Bath Road. The elephants had to walk and the village children would get buns from Mr Frederick Rosier, the Chapel Street baker, to feed them with.

Another trader in the street was Mr Harry Colburn, who kept a little butcher's shop adjoining the (old) Wheatsheaf public house. He paid a penny for a bucket of household scraps and rinds to feed to his pigs – it was a good way for children to raise money to spend on sweets. Their favourite Chapel Street shop was Franklin's, located in a row of houses called Park View. 'We used to get ten aniseed balls for 1d. and a liquorice shoelace for a farthing', Ivy recalled.

Thatcham then had a number of milkmen and Joe especially remembered Mr William Clarke of Chapel Street. He delivered milk in a churn on the back of a cart – if it was left unattended in the street, the children on their way to school were often tempted to turn on the tap and drink the milk. If the milkman returned unexpectedly, his milk was left flowing into the gutter!

The row of cottages where the Mace family lived then belonged to Colthrop Mill. 'Billy' Mace worked at the mill, in the chopping room where rags were shredded to make the paper. The cottage was old (like many others in Thatcham at that time) and quite primitive. It had an outside toilet and a well in the back garden.

In hot weather, butter and other perishable foods were put in a bucket and lowered down the well to keep them cool. When a copper was installed in the cottage to help with the washing the weekly rent was increased by 6d. to pay for it.

Joe Mace remembered that the summer of 1921 was particularly hot and dry. Drinking water became such valuable commodity that his father padlocked the lid of the well at night. Across on The Marsh (Dunstan Green) the drought made the ground split open 'just as if there had been an earthquake'. In wetter times, Ivy remembered collecting frog-spawn in the pond on The Marsh. Both had pleasant memories of the fair, which set up on The Marsh each autumn in those days.

At that time, homes in the village were supplied with gas from the Thatcham Gas Works in Station Road. The gas works was then managed by Mr Joseph Corderoy (manager 1902–30) and his son Tommy (manager 1930–36) – it was the latter who came round periodically to empty the domestic meters. The gas cost only 1d. per unit and lasted well, even if it did smell 'vile'.

The village streets were also illuminated with gas then, and a Mr Hyde was employed to go around the parish with a ladder, lighting the lamps in the evening and extinguishing them in the morning. Almost opposite the gas works, at the bottom of the Broadway, was the woodturnery works of Messrs John Brown and Sons. The timber they used was brought from estates at Bucklebury and Tidmarsh by horse and cart.

Thatcham High Street looking east around the time of the First World War with a crowd assembled at the top of the Broadway – reason unknown.

The view east along London Road past Dunstan Green (left) where – in the drought of 1921 – Joe Mace recalled the ground cracking open!

The thatched cottages in Chapel Street around 1912 – as a boy, Joe Mace's favourite shop in the street was Franklin's sweetshop.

Joe Mace still had vivid memories of the firm's employee, Mr Collins, setting off at the crack of dawn with a team of shire horses to bring back a load of timber for the woodturnery. When he left school, Joe went to work for another local woodturnery, that of Messrs Collins & Witts, where he spent his entire working life.

His sister Ivy went to work at Colthrop Mill when she grew up and was employed in the bag room there with two dozen or so other local women. In later life, she and brother Joe looked back over the years, having seen many changes in Thatcham. 'We used to know everybody, from one end of the village to the other', they reminisced, a claim that could never be made in the Thatcham of today!

A Coronation Celebration

Thatcham has grown enormously in the postwar years, but it may have lost something in the process – its strong sense of community. Local events drew a proportionately larger measure of support from the inhabitants in pre-war years. The celebrations here for the coronation of King George VI just before the last war, are a good illustration of this. George VI's coronation took place on Wednesday 12 May 1937, and the whole country rejoiced.

In Thatcham, the celebrations commenced at 7a.m. with a 'salute' by anvils in the Broadway. Anvil salutes on special occasions were an old Thatcham custom and this one was arranged by Arthur Brown whose family owned a garage in the Broadway. This was followed by an open-air service on the green, conducted by the Revd Daniel (of St Mary's Church) and the Revd Richmond (of the Congregational Church).

Crowds filled the Broadway and joined in enthusiastically with the opening hymn, 'All people that on earth do dwell'. The British Legion parade was led by their chairman and marshall, Mr W.J. Paterson. The houses and shops in Thatcham were all prettily decorated for the occasion, reflecting the patriotic fervour of the inhabitants.

Later in the morning, at 10a.m., the inhabitants of Thatcham watched the crowning of their 'Queen of the May', Miss Winifred Hall. Accompanied by the Thatcham band, resplendent in new uniforms, she entered the Broadway and mounted a platform erected there for the purpose. The 'Queen' was attended by five 'Maids of Honour' – Misses Fowler, Denness, Wyatt, Headlong and Page.

The village doctor, James Beagley, crowned Miss Hall. Dr Beagley made a short speech in which he expressed the hope that the May Queen's 'reign' would be a happy and joyful one. 'Though your reign be but for a day', he said, 'may good fortune prosper you all the days of your life'. Miss Hall responded with a charming little speech in which

she thanked the people of Thatcham for her reception:

I hereby declare that it is my earnest desire that everybody be happy and that they celebrate this day in manner befitting the coronation of the King and Queen.

Coronation Day 1937 commenced in Thatcham with an open-air service on the Broadway green conducted by Revd A.O. Daniel (foreground).

Coronation celebrations in Thatcham Broadway on 12 May 1937 – the ancient parish custom of anvil firing.

During Coronation Day 1937 the village May Queen (Miss Winifred Hall) toured Thatcham on the back of a lorry loaned by TRTS.

After this, the May Queen and her retinue toured the main streets of Thatcham on the back of a lorry loaned by TRTS (Thatcham Road Transport Services), which had been colourfully decorated for the occasion. The general feeling among the crowds was that the May Queen show was 'the best and prettiest thing ever seen in Thatcham'.

Coronation Day 1937 was intended for the crowning of King Edward VIII but he had abdicated at the end of the previous year. So it was actually King George VI and Queen Elizabeth who were crowned in Westminster Abbey. The BBC broadcast the coronation 'live' to the nation and in Thatcham it was relayed to hundreds of people who had gathered in the Broadway through two loudspeakers – a sign of the times, to be sure.

Prizes were given for the best decorations by judges who toured the village and inspected the houses and shops. Ten prizes were awarded altogether: first prize for the best decorated house went to No.88 Chapel Street, whilst the best shop was judged to be Mr Charles Pazzard's ironmongery in the High Street.

Commencing at 3p.m. in the afternoon, the local children performed on the Broadway green – almost everyone in the village came to watch. The programme, which lasted for nearly two hours, included maypole dancing, singing and physical training displays. Youngsters from the National,

Council and Infant schools participated, and the Council School's older boys – all dressed in white flannels – performed a special physical training display.

By 5p.m. the 500 school children had earned their reward and went off either to the Parish Hall or the British School for tea. Both places were visited by Winifred Hall, the May Queen. The Council Junior School had chosen its own 'Queen', little June Patterson, aged five years. At 6p.m., Miss Hall presented prizes to the winners of the various competitions and then led a procession to the football field. Here, hundreds of spectators watched the antics of Joe Lovelock's 'comic sportsmen'.

Back in the Broadway, the crowds listened to the King's speech on the loudspeakers. At 9p.m. some 2,000 people – nearly half the population of Thatcham – crowded onto the green to watch a tableau. Written by Mr Hugh Mytton, 'A Dream of Empire' was narrated by Dr Beagley.

After the first two scenes, however, torrential rain sent everyone scurrying for shelter. Fortunately, it did not prevent the final act in the day's proceedings, a 'coronation bonfire' on Dunstan Green.

The *Newbury Weekly News* carried a report of Thatcham's coronation celebration which concluded that '… never has the parish risen to the occasion in such an enthusiastic and whole-hearted manner' – a compliment indeed to Thatcham in the 1930s!

Chapter VII

People and Places: Part Two

Thatcham Folk in Days Gone By

Memories of life in Old Thatcham were recalled in an interview 20 years ago, by Mrs Beatrice Jones (née Heaver) who was born at Thatcham Newtown (St John's Road) in 1908. Her father, Mr Frederick Heaver, was employed by John Brown & Sons at their woodturnery works in the Broadway, where he was a circular saw operator.

In the days before rubbish collections were made in the village, many Newtown folk threw theirs into the 'tip' (where Thatcham Children's Centre is today). Mrs Jones remembered her father taking the family rubbish there in a wheelbarrow – as refuse then included ashes from coal fires, the 'tip' smouldered continuously, even after it was covered over.

The rest of that area was then meadowland where cows were put out to graze. A small herd was kept by Mr John Adams, whose house was then the only habitation in Lower Way. He ran the Crown Acre Dairy and went round the village every morning with his milk cart. 'A cheerful soul', he was always very smart with his gaiters 'polished to perfection' and 'a rose-bud in his button-hole' in the summer.

From a large churn, he dispensed milk into pint and half-pint jugs to customers who met him at their doors and paid him on the spot. Sadly, he was taken ill on his rounds one day in 1926 and died soon afterwards but his son Frank kept the family business going.

Amongst other Thatcham businesses of that period was one located at Newtown – Messrs Carter's, the 'oldest rope and sack manufactory in Berkshire'. The firm specialised in making driving belts for farm machinery and waterproof cloths for wagons and hayricks in their premises, which extended through to Green Lane.

In the 1920s, the proprietor was Mr Albert Carter who lived at Newtown House (12 Bath Road). His daughter, Miss Kate Carter LRAM – 'a fine musician' – gave piano lessons which could often be seen (and heard) with her pupils in the front room of the house.

Along in Thatcham village proper were traders such as Mr Bernard Brooks, the corn chandler. Although he had premises in the High Street and a corn store in Park Lane, he lived at Coombe Lodge in Chapel Street (where Coombe Court is today). 'Ever active in public life', he is remembered as one of the original members of Thatcham Parish Council.

A little way down the High Street was the draper's shop (No.25) kept by Mr Alfred Gibbs, a ladies' and gents' complete outfitters, which stocked 'genuine goods at the lowest prices'. Even further down, on the other side of the road, was a toy shop (No.34) kept by Mrs Maude Adams.

She was a 'dear old lady' who sold toys of every

The Bath Road at Thatcham Newtown looking east – Beatrice Jones (née Heaver) was born in St John's Road (off to the right) *in 1908 and spent her childhood here.*

Above: *The High Street looking west in the 1930s – here were many of the village shops, and the post office, remembered by Beatrice Jones from her younger days in Thatcham.*

Left: *Chapel Street looking east in the 1930s – opposite the thatched cottages was Coombe Lodge, where Mr Bernard Brooks, the corn chandler lived.*

description – her prices started at 1d. for a pencil – and the stock ranged through colouring books and paints, tops and hoops, to dolls and dolls' prams. 'It was like an Aladdin's cave to us poor children', recalled Mrs Jones.

The High Street was the location of Thatcham's post office for many years although it occupied different premises. In the 1920s, it was on the south side of the street at No.35. Officially, the sub-postmaster was Mr Basil Gilmour, although his wife was usually in charge there, with a staff of two lady counter assistants.

Highlights of the year for village children included magic lantern shows at the British School in Church Lane. Held in the winter, just before Christmas, they usually had a 'temperance' theme and showed a poor woman and her children, with no food to eat because her husband had spent all the money on drink. Each child was given an orange and an apple to take home.

In the summer there was an annual outing to Padworth House, organised by the White Ribboners, a local temperance group. Children travelled by train to Aldermaston Station and then walked through the lanes to the house, where trestle tables were set out with 'all sorts of goodies'. There were games and races, and then the train journey back to Thatcham.

Of all her memories, those which Mrs Jones treasured most were of her schooldays. She joined the Council School when it opened in 1913 and remembers the headmaster Mr Horatio Skillman and his staff of four lady teachers, the Misses Pearce, Peters, Pinnock and Ashman. Rhoda Pearce died in 1921 having been 'for 40 years a teacher of little children in this village'.

She also remembered many of the (then) children who she went to school with during the First World War period, such as Stanley King (whose father kept the Crown pub in the High Street), Ned Lawrence (who emigrated to New Zealand), and Philip Coleman (who became a policeman in Hong Kong).

In her own adulthood, Mrs Jones married a London man: she recalled her combined 21st birthday and engagement party in 1929 fondly. That morning, the family baker arrived with a long baking tin full of lardy-cakes as a gift on her special day! Of three village bakers at that time, her family were customers of Mr Cruse, who had a shop in Station Road.

He went round the village with a horse and cart, calling door to door with a basket of bread from which customers made their choice. 'My mother was particularly fond of a cottage loaf and the more burnt the bottom part the more she liked it'.

Mrs Jones – as she now was – left Thatcham to go and live in London but came home every summer to visit during the 1930s, being evacuated back to her family home when war broke out in 1939. Returning to 'the country' after living in London highlighted the rather primitive domestic facilities village homes then had. 'We had an outside toilet which was on mains sewerage system but we had no cistern', she recalled. 'So a bucket of water was kept there and whoever used it was responsible for bringing it indoors and filling it again'.

Water was originally taken from a pump in the scullery – 'it was that cold it was a joy to drink' – but when mains water arrived in the 1930s it was not so nice yet added 3d. a week to the rent. Electricity was installed in the house for the landlord by the Wessex Electricity Company – 'two lights, one in the kitchen and one in the front room' – but that added another shilling a week to the rent.

Mrs Jones remembered Mr Gilbert, the Chapel Street cycle agent. During the war, her husband sent a gent's cycle down to Thatcham for their son, then aged nine. It was too big for the boy, who couldn't reach the pedals, so she took it along to Mr Gilbert to see if he could help. He fitted thick pieces of wood to the pedals and 'hey presto, that did the trick'.

On another occasion, she had cycled with her son and daughter to tea with friends at Woolhampton. On the return journey, her daughter's bike got a puncture, which meant a long walk home. 'Along comes a car, stops, and out gets Mr Gilbert to ask what the trouble was'. He put bike and rider in his car, transported both back to Thatcham and fixed the puncture at his shop – 'just a little story of his kindness to all and sundry', commented Mrs Jones.

Thatcham in the 1930s

More childhood memories of Thatcham in the 1930s were recalled for me in interviews with a lady and two brothers who grew up in the old village.

Mrs Rose Bellis (née Goodman) whose family home in the 1930s was one house in a row since demolished (where Elms Avenue is situated today), on the south side of Chapel Street. She believed that the property then belonged to Colthrop Mill, where her father worked.

Her father, Mr Albert Goodman, was employed at Colthrop Mill for over half a century. Like many other employees, he worked shifts – 12 hours on days, then 12 hours on nights, alternately – and was paid just over £2 per week in the 1930s. Of this, he

'Gentlemen Jim' (James) Matthews outside his grocery shop in Chapel Street in the 1930s – Rose Bellis lived off this street as a child and recalled many of the shops which once traded here.

The Broadway green looking north in the 1930s – on the west side of the green lived Mrs Upfold who kept an indiscreet parrot outside her door!

paid around 5s. a week in rent.

As a child, Mrs Bellis remembered Chapel Street well and had pleasant memories of the place. She recalled visits to Mrs Emily Nightingale's sweetshop (No.34) on her way to school, a favourite with local children. Among the treats to be had was 'a chocolate coconut square for one farthing!'

Then there was Frederick Rosier's bakery (No.76), from which bread was delivered by a roundsman, on foot, with a large basket on his arm. 'Mum always had a cottage loaf', recalled Mrs Bellis, so that Dad could take the top to work, to eat – with a lump of cheese and onion – for his lunch.

Of local characters at this period, she especially recalled an old man who also lived in Chapel Street and who was known as 'Shalligo' as far as she was aware. Eventually, she discovered that this was only a nick-name, given to him because of his indecisiveness – going out was always a problem for him because he could never make up his mind what to do, saying to himself 'shall I go, or shan't I?'.

Around in the Broadway, Mrs Bellis remembered

'an old fish lady called Mrs Upfold', who lived on the west side of the green. This lady kept a parrot outside her door: the bird could talk but had no sense of propriety, calling out 'Here comes the old b....., Mother' as the vicar walked by!

Brothers Bert and Ted Chandler lived in Henwick Lane and attended St Mary's School in Park Lane as schoolboys. Their out-of-school memories of Thatcham in the 1930s focused on local shops, particularly those that sold sweets. There was Mrs Rufey's bow-windowed 'provision store' (No.19) in the Broadway – which also sold groceries and cigarettes – and Mrs Elizabeth Randall's 'little old sweetshop' (No.29, today a tyre depot) in the High Street.

Bert Chandler remembered the old-fashioned 'English drug store' (chemists) kept by Mr Thomas Oakeley (at No.1, High Street). It was a slightly eerie place to visit as a child, with a high counter and shelves lined with coloured jars – orange, red and green – from which the medicines were mixed. The shop also sold patent medicines and proprietory articles. This business had a competitor too, in the form of Mr Charles Bevan's 'chemist and druggists' (at No.33).

Elsewhere in the High Street, Mrs Maud Adams ran a grocery shop and refreshment rooms (at No.34). Also in the High Street was the hairdressing shop kept by Mr Tommy King (No.27). He took on an apprentice named Bill Hall, who later set up his own 'Gents' and boys' hairdressing salon' nearby. So the one-time pupil became a competitor, the brothers recalled.

Much the same thing had happened with Mr Maurice House: he had learned his trade with Mr Henry Mayers – 'Builder, Contractor and Undertaker' of No.79 Bath Road. Then he went into partnership with Mr Herbert Denness and the pair set up as carpenters and decorators, doing business from their workshop in Park Lane.

The view north up Park Lane – Bert and Ted Chandler recalled Messrs House and Denness' carpentry and decorating business having their workshop here.

More Thatcham Schooldays Remembered

One gentleman who shared his recollections of life in Thatcham in the 1930s was Mr George Slade, who was born in 1921 at Lower Farm, Greenham, but whose family soon afterwards moved to Dunstan Green where he grew up.

His schooldays were spent first at the Infant School in the Broadway, under the headmistress Miss Blanche Green and teacher Miss Gertie Bosley. He later transferred to the National School in Park Lane, where the headmaster was Mr Aubrey Chapman. As a senior boy, he was entrusted with the sale of produce from the school garden, where vegetables were grown using a 'crop rotation' system.

Thatcham in the 1930s was a relatively quiet place and offered little for young people to do. However, there were some clubs, such as those run by Miss Millicent Turner (of Thatcham House in Station Road) at the Parish Hall, and Miss Marjorie Brown (of Wetherdene in Park Lane) at her preparatory school. In the paddock here, village boys and girls learned to play tennis.

Of course, there were also football and cricket clubs in Thatcham at that time. As a boy, George Slade remembers playing football on Dunstan Green but he went on to become captain of the Thatcham Minors (under-16) team. The team's first-ever season was 1937/8 and was very successful for the youngsters – they won the Newbury Minor League Cup. The team trainer was Mr Bert Parker.

As a schoolboy, Mr Slade earned pocket money by doing three newspaper delivery rounds, mornings, evenings and Sundays. His morning round was done for Mr Wilfrid Fuller, who had a newsagent's shop (now Crayden's) in the Broadway. The evening round was undertaken for Mr Anthony Stacchini, whose shop was in the High Street (and was later kept by newsagent Mr Norman Hall).

The evening newspapers were collected by Mr Slade from Thatcham railway station, then in the charge of stationmaster Mr Arthur Arch. The newspapers were in bundles which were 'thrown' from the train as it passed through the station, from where they were ferried by bicycle to Mr Stacchini's shop. Here, they were sold over the counter or delivered around the village by George Slade.

On leaving school at the age of 14, Mr Slade went to work for Florco at Colthrop. He earned 18s.9d. for a five-day-week and thinks that the average weekly wage of an adult labourer was about £2.5s.0d. in the 1930s. In later years, Mr Slade set up on his own as a plasterer and met Mr Jim Cope, a skilled craftsman who left his trademark (a pheasant drawing) on his building work around the village.

In the 1930s, the carton-making firm Cropper's of Colthrop had a sports field adjacent to Dunstan

Thatcham High Street looking east in the 1930s, showing the original junction with Park Lane (left) – this is a view of the village as George Slade knew it when he was a young man.

The Thatcham Minors Football Team of 1937/8. Left to right, back row: Charlie Seymour, Ken Bartholomew, Jack Davies, Les Arnold, Gordon Barr; front row: Peter House, Jack Brooks, George Slade, Percy Davies, Stan Dennis; on the floor: Max Goddard, Russell Hunt; adults: Freddie Davies and Bert Parker.

The view across Dunstan Green in the 1930s – George Slade recalled playing football here as a boy. He also remembered the splendid annual village fêtes held on this green in the 1930s.

Green and this was the site of the splendid village fêtes then put on annually. Admission cost only 6d. but there were numerous attractions, such as dirt track riders, military bands, fancy dress competitions and even a visit from the celebrated Dagenham Girl Pipers – a feast of entertainment!

The organisation of these fêtes was largely the work of Mr Keith Brooks and his brother Bertie. They were the sons of Mr Bernard Brooks, the High Street corn merchant. The family lived at Coombe Lodge in Chapel Street (where Coombe Court is today). They had a grain store at the end of Park Lane, whilst in a field alongside their house they kept a herd of prize-winning Aberdeen Angus cattle.

Next door lived Mr Alec Rose, who kept a market garden and sold flowers. Among many other old Chapel Street residents recalled by George Slade were Mr Albert Attwood, who kept the New Inn (later the Prancing Horse but now no longer a pub) at No.49 Chapel Street and Mr Bill Nightingale, who had a sweetshop at No.34 Chapel Street.

As far as is known, the latter was not related to Mrs Emily Nightingale and her daughter Ruby, who ran a grocery-cum-newsagents-cum-sweetshop at the second house just east of Stoney Lane (today a restaurant). But there were others of that surname at that time – Mr Frederick Nightingale was also a shopkeeper, at Colthrop. So there were a number of Nightingales in and around 1930s Thatcham!

How Gilbert Court Got Its Name

Not everyone with memories of old Thatcham was born in the place. Some came to the village in adult life, such as Mr and Mrs Gilbert, who came to the village, making it their adopted home, and leaving their mark on the place.

Mr Leslie Frank Gilbert was born in Hertfordshire in 1898 whilst his wife, Constance Isabel, was born in Chelsea in 1899, the eldest of five sisters. The couple met whilst working at a factory in London and married in the summer of 1931, moving to Thatcham soon after. Mr Gilbert was a distant relative of Charlie Clark, who owned three tiny cottages (Nos 4, 6 and 8) and a shop (No.10) in Chapel Street.

Mr and Mrs Gilbert travelled down to Thatcham by motorcycle and their first impression of the village was that it was 'a lovely little place'. For a few weeks the couple lodged with Frank Ashman, the local saddler and bootmaker, at his home in Park Lane. Before the year was out, Leslie Gilbert succeeded Roland French as the proprietor of the cycle shop at No.10 Chapel Street and the couple moved into the premises.

At first, Mrs Gilbert found life in the village rather primitive. She took a pride in her cooking but had only a small scullery at the back of the shop, with just a single gas ring to cook on. Later, a small gas stove

The Gilberts' shop at No.10 Chapel Street in the 1930s – Leslie and Connie Gilbert are standing in the doorway. Their main trade was cycle sales but they also sold wirelesses and gramophones.

Members of Thatcham WI at their 40th Anniversary Dinner in October 1978. Left to right: Mrs Stanton, Mrs Flitter, Mrs Cooper, Mrs Hague, Mrs Craggs, Mrs Flatman (president), Mrs Gilbert (founder member), Mrs Dowd, Mrs Read.

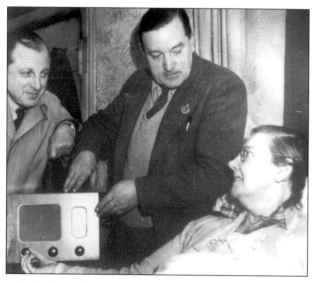

Mr Leslie Gilbert presenting a radio to old Thatcham resident Mrs Bessie Broughton in the 1950s.

was installed but the smell of the 'Thatcham gas' (supplied from the local gasworks in Station Road) was 'vile'. She also enjoyed singing, being a member of the Congregational Church choir for many years.

Mains water was just then being laid on in Thatcham but families living on the north side of Chapel Street still drew their water from wells and pumps fed by a stream –'it never ran dry', recalled Mrs Gilbert. Today, she is remembered as a good speaker and someone who always spoke her mind. Her strong Christian beliefs and principles, combined with a sense of humour and concern for others, earned her much respect from locals of all ages.

Among the other folk in Chapel Street in the 1930s were William and Frank Woodbridge, two brothers who ran a dairy farm (at No.2). Along the road was

Fred Joyce's hardware store (No.50), renowned for offering 'a hundred and one ideas'. Further down was George Pike, blacksmith, from whose workshop door (No.64) floated a strong smell of combustion. Towards the end of the street was the shop (No.86) kept by James Hanson, who also went round the village streets selling vegetables from his 'coster's barrow'.

From their own shop, the Gilberts sold new and second hand bicycles and undertook cycle repairs. They also traded in wireless and gramophones, accumulators and records. Leslie Gilbert had his own public address system, which he took to local fêtes and often set up in the Broadway (plugging into the electricity supply from Charles Whitehouse's jewellery shop there). Radio broadcasts from London were thus relayed to the villagers who gathered round to listen.

Mrs Gilbert was a founder member of Thatcham Women's Institute, set up in 1938 (she was secretary for ten years and then president). They met at the Parish Hall, holding speaker meetings and musical sessions, at which Miss Eva Fyfield regularly played the piano. Mr Gilbert handled all bookings for the Parish Hall, opposite his shop, and became a member of the village recreation grounds committee.

The Gilberts were also involved in the founding of Thatcham Old People's Welfare (now Age Concern). Their shop was an informal meeting place for folk concerned with the welfare of Thatcham's needy, including Nurse Slade, who lived in the (then) new nurse's house in Church Gate. She is remembered as a stout lady – a typical district nurse – and a 'dear old soul'.

When the war broke out in 1939, the Gilberts took in evacuees and relatives from London. They had no children of their own but took care of three of Mr Gilbert's cousin's children – Heather, Hazel and

Rosemary – who stayed in Thatcham after the war finished. Throughout the war, Mrs Gilbert and other WI members devoted their time to canning surplus fruit and vegetables to sell at meetings.

After the war, the couple remained active in village life. Mrs Gilbert had fond memories of the Thatcham Amateur Variety Artistes – amongst them Albert Phillips, the Broadway baker, 'with his fine bass voice' – who performed along at the Drill Hall. Mr Gilbert's main hobby was golf, and he joined the Newbury and Crookham Golf Club, but he was also a member of Thatcham's British Legion and did a great deal of social service work in the village. Sadly, he died in 1972.

Mrs Gilbert's work for Thatcham WI was honoured with an invitation to a Buckingham Palace garden party. A more lasting recognition of the couple's dedication to Thatcham was the naming of Gilbert Court, on the Bath Road, after them – it was opened by Mrs Gilbert in October 1975. The good lady herself died in 1991 but she was always proud of Thatcham, the place she and her husband adopted as 'their village' many years before.

The Good Old Days Of Thatcham Past

These recollections of life in the old village were supplied by the late Mr Cyril Muttram and his wife Agnes (née Collins). The couple lived in Hartmead Road at the time they offered these reminiscences. They recalled what Thatcham was like in the 1920s and 1930s, when it was still very much a close-knit community.

Mr Muttram's family roots were actually in Devon, but his father – George – found employment as a fitter at Colthrop Mill in 1911. It was at this time that a machine was moved from Ivybridge to Colthrop and installed here to make felt for floorcloth. At this date the mill made vast quantities of paper bags, chiefly brown and blue bags as used by grocers and the other purveyors – the manufacture of bags then consumed half of all the paper produced by Colthrop Mill and provided work for many local women who pasted them together.

The Muttram family lived at the canalside colony of Colthrop Cottages, where Cyril was born in 1918. At the age of 14 he went to work in the mill as a carpenter and joiner. In fact, his whole family was eventually employed at the mill. He also served as a part-time fireman with the mill's own fire brigade, as did his father and brothers. One brother – Wilf – became welfare officer at Colthrop Mill in later years. Cyril Muttram was employed at the mill for 36 years, before retiring because of ill-health; sadly, he died in 1996.

Mrs Muttram (née Collins) was born in the Broadway, where she spent the early years of her life right at the centre of the old village. Her family lived

for a time in an old cottage (one of two, now demolished) at the bottom of the Broadway, opposite the Old Chequers pub, at the front of what was then Messrs John Brown & Sons' woodturnery works. She was able to recall how the firm's employees brought loads of timber into the works by horse and cart – not least because one of them was her own father, Mr Edwin 'Ernest' Collins!

Joe Lovelock helped with this work and – like her father – 'was very good with horses'. She was able to recall other employees at the woodturnery in those days: Tommy Cousens and Bert Nightingale worked in the Japanning shop, applying coloured lacquers to brush handles; Dan Dance worked in the chair-making shop (above the main factory); Johnny Hunt was kept busy selling sacks of off-cuts for firewood; and a Mr Tigwell tended the steam engine, in the boiler room, providing power for the lathes and other machinery.

The Broadway – then the hub of village life – comprised a mixture of shops and houses. Mrs

Agnes Muttram (née Collins) was born in the Thatcham Broadway and spent the early years of her life in the old village centre, seen here as it was in the days of her childhood.

Thatcham Broadway looking north in the 1930s – Mrs Muttram recalled Fred Spanswick, local bus proprietor, who kept his vehicle in a yard at the end of an alleyway (off to the left).

The view from the Broadway into the High Street – in the 1930s Lionel Baker kept the butcher's shop nearby, which Mrs Muttram remembered from her younger days.

Thatcham's Disappearing Depot

Thatcham's ex-Army depot site has become the latest of Thatcham's vast housing estates. Anyone travelling down Station Road today may find it hard to recall that Thatcham Depot once stood here. Now, virtually nothing remains as a reminder of the fact that six decades of local history were played out at the Depot and that literally hundreds of local people worked here over the years.

Two of those people were Mr and Mrs Stanbrook of Lancaster Close. Jointly, the couple gave some 60 years' service to the Depot. They retired together in 1987. Bill Stanbrook had worked there continuously since 1958 – his wife Jean was employed there from 1952, even before they married, although her service was broken as they raised a family. Between them, they have fond memories of their time at the Depot, recalling how some locals regarded it as a 'holiday camp' whereas it was 'really hard work', although there was a great sense of camaraderie.

Having been requisitioned by the Army, the Depot opened as such in February 1940. Its first commanding officer was Lt Col V.W. Urquart MC. It was taken over by the United States Army in November 1942, and became General Depot 45. The largest G-Depot in this country, G-45 carried stores and supplies of all types; scores of storage sheds were erected and 35 miles of railway sidings put in, extending across Thatcham Moors to Newbury Racecourse. The Depot was at its peak around D-Day in June 1944, when there were 7,000 people working there. By 1946 there were still over 8,000 soldiers and 600 civilian employees at the Depot, as well as nearly 2,000 prisoners of war (many of whom had been held in Thatcham since 1944). G-45 was the last G-Depot to close after the war, being handed back by the Americans to the British in May 1946. The Army continued to use the Depot as a storage and distribution base, and sent huge quantities of equipment here for reconditioning. For example, in the immediate postwar years, consignments of used gas masks arrived in Thatcham to be reconditioned and re-issued.

When Jean started work at the Depot in 1952, 'anti-gas' was still vital work. Gas masks came into the Depot for checking and were then sent to B Shed (one of the holding sheds), for eventual re-issue. This particular work slowly declined, and 'after the gas masks finished', she recalls, the Depot turned its attention to a variety of equipment – 'everything that needed reconditioning'. Her career there began in C Shed, on tent and clothing repair. The work in this shed included the waterproofing of tents and ropes, which were then transferred to A Shed until required.

It was not until 1958 that Bill started work at the Depot. He had been disabled with polio the year before but approached Lt Col Farnaby, who interviewed him and gave him a job. Initially, he too

Muttram remembered the names of the occupants of almost every one in the 1930s, including the fresh fish shop (No.12) run by George Vass (previously Martin's, pork butchers), plus two shops now demolished – the fish and chip shop (No.1) established by Aubrey Collins (no relation) and, opposite, the boot repair shop (No.61) kept by Frank Ashman.

Further down the Broadway (where the Co-operative supermarket is today) lived Fred Spanswick who was the local bus proprietor. His only vehicle, a single decker, was parked in a yard at the end of an alleyway when not in use. By day, it plied to and from Newbury – Arthur Amor was a regular driver in the 1930s, Mrs Muttram recalled. On the last bus back to Thatcham each evening, especially when there had been a market or fair in Newbury, the passengers 'had a lot of laughs' in the days of a close-knit community.

Back at the top of the Broadway was a butcher's shop (Nos 7–8), which traded as Wyatt's, having been established by Robert Wyatt in about 1892, although it was run by Lionel Baker in the 1930s. At this time of year, all the shops in and around the Broadway decorated their windows with holly and paper chains but Wyatt's went one better – turkeys and pheasants were hung up on display outside. They ended up on Christmas dinner tables: 'Of course, it wouldn't be allowed today', Mrs Muttram acknowledged.

On Boxing Day, a popular event in the village was a fancy dress football match. The participants assembled in the Broadway and walked to a meadow in Park Lane where they played a seasonal game before a crowd of spectators. In the post-Christmas period there were also pantomimes in the British School, playing to packed houses and enjoyed by performers and audience alike. Mrs Muttram thought the sense of community in the modern town of Thatcham seemed to have dwindled since the good old days.

The Gatehouse at the Depot, viewed from Station Road in operational days – today the access road to yet another of Thatcham's vast housing estates.

One of the Depot's annual September sports days in the postwar years – this one in 1947.

The same event – the sports days were shared by civilian spectators as well as military personnel.

A group photo showing the Depot's 'admin' (office) staff c.1990.

Also c.1990, a group photo of the Depot's (shed) storage personnel.

A view of the interior of the Officers' Mess, probably on the occasion of Christmas dinner, 1990.

worked in C Shed and recalls a workforce there of some 300 women, half a dozen men and up to 20 other disabled employees like himself. He later transferred to D Shed (stationery), which had workshops dealing with a variety of tasks (such as carpentry, blacksmithing, signwriting and textiles), where he was employed mostly on materials salvage for the rest of his service.

Up to this period, the Depot was still employing up to a 1000 people, mostly civilians from Thatcham and the surrounding area. There were more servicemen at the Depot early on, including lesser ranks (from Hermitage), although the number fell as the years passed – but those in charge were mostly Army officers. Amongst the senior officers at one time were a Col Bangham and a Major Gunn. The latter liked a tipple, and reputedly often carried a bottle of whisky in his pocket, which got him dismissed, giving rise to the story that 'Colonel Bangham fired Major Gunn!'

Whilst the wages at the Depot were only modest for most employees – Bill Stanbrook started on £7.16s. a week as a stores assistant in 1958 – it was able to attract workers, and men laid off by Colthrop Mill relocated there. Working conditions sometimes left much to be desired and the massive sheds were often cold. Early on, the only heating was from wood-burning stoves and the workers spent a lot of time chopping up

palettes for fuel to keep warm – all day long in winter. Later, warm air blowers were installed but didn't work, apparently blowing out cold air.

The Depot had its own fire station, complete with tender, and its own railway sidings leading off the main line, complete with its own steam engine and engine shed. Jean later worked in 'traffic', recalling that incoming railway trucks of materials had to be dealt with in a day or a 'demurrage charge' was levied on the Depot by British Railways. Although there was a canteen for the employees, Bill remembers that few employees used it and instead bought food and drink from the refreshment tractor and trailer that plied around the 1½ miles of perimeter road daily.

Up until 1964, buses ferried in the large workforce from miles away but after that date the number of employees began to decline as the Depot's operations were cut back. It still provided equipment for the Royal Tournament and Bisley, and overseas campaigns like the Falklands, but its days were numbered. Its closure was confirmed in 1998 and the 232 civilian jobs still based there were to go. It did not close officially until March 2000, although the last 'Beating of the Retreat' was held in December 1999 and by that date, Bill and Jean Stanbrook had been retired for 12 years.

Chapter VIII
The Rise and Fall of Colthrop Mill

Cropper's Comes to Colthrop

The origins of Colthrop Mill date back to at least 1421, when it was a 'grist' (corn) mill, and records show that it had become a 'fulling' (cloth) mill by 1540. However, two centuries later it had become a paper mill, although it remained a small-scale concern until it was acquired in 1861 by Mr John Henry, under whose ownership its modern history began.

He faced many difficulties but successfully developed and expanded Colthrop paper mill. He also opened up a sales office in London. At this time a large number of paper bags were made at Colthrop, chiefly brown paper and sugar bags as used by grocers, drapers and warehousemen – this formed half of all the paper made at Colthrop.

The Henry family made several technical improvements at Colthrop Mill. In the year 1894 too, they installed a new 170h.p. gas engine at the mill to drive the pulp beaters – it was guaranteed to use less than

half the coal of the old steam engine! However, in old age, John Henry's health began to decline and he went to Bath to convalesce in 1905.

He died there at the age of 82. He left four daughters and three sons, two of whom took over the firm – John M. (Jack) at Colthrop and Matthew in London. The brothers continued to make innovations. During 1908 they bought a paper mill at Lee Mill Bridge in Devon. When this mill later closed, the machine there was moved to Colthrop.

By the time of the First World War – under the sons of John Henry – Colthrop's paper mill had become an industrial success story – and so there were now others prepared to take the business on. It was still a family firm at this date, under the control of brothers John Maclean ('Jack') and Matthew Henry, but as such its days were numbered.

Meanwhile, in many ways the production of paper at Colthrop Mill went on as before. Although a gas engine had been installed, it only replaced the mill's waterwheel as a source of power for the pulp beaters

Left: *Colthrop Mill, with female employees visible, as seen from the canal at Colthrop Lock, c.1900.*

Below: *Colthrop Mill looking west from the canal bank in 1907 – the swing bridge linked the mill with Colthrop Cottages.*

– it did not fully supersede the mill's steam engines, which were still required to boil rags, drive the paper machine and dry the paper.

Sadly, whilst the gas engine possessed 'all the latest new patents' and in 1894 was 'one of the largest yet made', it exploded in 1914, killing millwright Fred Wise who was trying to repair it. Both the mill's steam and gas engines were fuelled by coal, which was brought in by canal before the mill's first railway siding was installed in 1915.

During the war, however, Colthrop Mill supplied paper which, after laminating, was converted into cartons by a London firm named Cropper's. Mr Samuel Cropper had started this in 1879 and he had been making cardboard cartons with paper produced at Colthrop since then. After the war, the Colthrop Board & Paper Mills Ltd was established.

It was formed by an amalgamation of the Henry's family business and Samuel Cropper's London company in 1918. That year, alongside the existing paper mill, construction of a new board mill commenced – it began production in 1921. A further company, Containers Ltd, was formed in 1920 and accommodated in the new South Board Mill at Colthrop. It made folding cardboard cases on a 1,600h.p. machine purchased from Black-Clawson.

Even in 1920 the mill was still using 150 tons of coal a week. During the miners' strike of April–June, 1921, a shortage of coal resulted in most of the mill's machinery being shut down. Of the 375 men and 100 women then employed at the mill, 300 employees had to be laid off – bag making continued, mostly undertaken by women workers. But change was imminent.

The South Board Mill was a huge new factory that offered employment for up to 600 workers. Cropper's proposed to move their entire operations from London to 'an industrial colony', having 'important influences on the future of Thatcham and the neighbouring town of Newbury'. Records indicate that the whole thing was well thought out.

'Accustomed as they are to the life and animation of a big city', it was realised that moving to a rural district like Thatcham 'these Londoners would not care to be cut off from all the social and recreational attractions of town life'. So the directors of Cropper's proposed to house many of the London workers not in Thatcham but in Newbury!

For example, Cropper's purchased a site in Clifton Road where they had soon built eight houses and were in negotiation with Newbury Corporation for acquiring the frontage of this housing site 'for the erection of some 20 houses to accommodate managers and foremen'. Colthrop could be reached either by bus, or train from Westfields Halt.

Cropper's London employees were offered the chance to see their new workplace when the firm's directors put on an excursion to Colthrop. Five coaches left London at 8a.m. and reached Colthrop

A unique photograph of the South Mill's steam engine in the charge of Mr Charles Lovegrove about 1920.

Colthrop Mill Fire Brigade's fire engine in the 1920s – a Leyland vehicle fitted with a Merryweather pump.

Mill at noon. Here, the visitors were shown around the mill, 'seeing the new machinery in operation' and getting 'a general view of the place'.

We are not told what these London employees thought of Colthrop Mill (or the locality) but the directors were effusive in their own praise of what was on offer. Here, the employees would 'work amidst plenty of light, plenty of elbow room, plenty of fresh air' – all of which was essential to making their work – more pleasant and congenial'.

So, in 1923, Cropper's moved their entire operations from Southwark to Colthrop, which was now home not just to the paper mill but also to Cropper's, which made light cardboard boxes, and to Containers, which made heavy cardboard products. (In 1927, Colthrop began manufacturing paper sacks but this work was transferred to Aylesford in Kent in 1932.)

Nevertheless, the industry still used combustible materials and the danger of fire remained. As early as May 1923, there was a big blaze at Colthrop Mill. A shed measuring 60x150 feet was totally destroyed in the conflagration. Having had a motor fire engine since 1913, Newbury Fire Brigade arrived on site sooner but not soon enough, so the mill management set up its own brigade.

'Cropper & Co. Ltd, Folding Box Manufacturers, Thatcham, Berks' – Colthrop Mill seen in an aerial view of the inter-war years.

Above: *An interior view of the Cropper's factory in 1923 – then known as 'Containers Ltd', it manufactured folding cardboard boxes.*

Left: *Another interior view of Cropper's factory in 1923. It shows the belt-driven machinery then used for printing the cardboard boxes.*

Just a few years later, there were two fires in the same year. In March 1926, a blaze broke out in a shed containing 1,000 tons of baled paper. Newbury Fire Brigade arrived there in just 18 minutes but their efforts to contain the fire were handicapped by darkness. Some 70 workers found themselves out of work temporarily, although 40 of them were engaged in a salvage operation.

In July 1926, there was another fire in a corrugated iron shed containing 400 tons of wood pulp. This time the Newbury Fire Brigade arrived in only 12 minutes but wind fanned the flames and the mill's fire pump soon broke down. With their 'steamer', the Newbury firemen damped down the smouldering fire for four days and the Colthrop board

machine was working again a day later.

A serious blaze occurred in May 1938, when fire broke out in a store shed containing nearly 3,000 tons of wood pulp, waste paper and newsprint. Smoke was spotted coming through the shed's roof and the mill fire engine was quickly on the scene. The Newbury Fire Brigade was also alerted and arrived in just 10 minutes, so that altogether there were four pumps dealing with the blaze.

By nightfall, the blaze was at its height and floodlights were set up to assist the firemens' efforts. Gradually, their efforts paid off and one Newbury pump left next morning, the other that afternoon. The fire was confined to the store shed but had been so fierce that steel supports had twisted in the heat

Colthrop Mill Fire brigade tackle a fire in the South Mill's waste shed on 6 September 1952 – the men's wives served them tea!

Colthrop Mill Fire Brigade in the late 1950s, with trophies they won in competitions. The officers include John Henry (managing director) and Stan Langford (chief fire officer).

Colthrop Mill employees enjoyed social occasions such as this – a Cropper's Christmas party for mill workers' families in 1951.

and over £15,000 worth of damage was done; however production was quickly resumed.

With the high levels of unemployment of the inter-war years, maintaining production at Colthrop mattered – it was a major local employer of men, women and boys. Paper and board were produced by both day and night shifts. The business prospered, and as a result the mill was extended and a second board machine installed there by Messrs Walmsleys Ltd of Bury (Lancashire) in 1939.

The outbreak of war in that year created some problems for the Colthrop complex. Containers' premises were requisitioned for use as a Royal Navy supplies store. An aircraft look-out point was set up on the roof of a waste shed and manned 24 hours a day – in July 1940, a German aircraft dropped 15 bombs along the railway line, one of which caused damage to the factory roof!

When Colthrop's male employees went off to war, more women than ever before were employed there, doing jobs they had never done before – one female employee drove a Lister truck, taking cardboard from the machines. Moreover, like factories across the country, Colthrop was obliged to fit its paper and board production alongside essential War Department work for the duration.

After the war, the industry in general went through a difficult patch but Colthrop fared relatively better. By the early 1950s, all parts of the business there were well in profit. Mr Frank W.J. Smith (the chairman and managing director of Colthrop Mill, Croppers' and Containers) reported that Colthrop was 'now working to full capacity and our order book could not be healthier'.

Shareholders were being paid dividends of over 27 per cent and not surprisingly sang the praises of the chairman and directors at company meetings. Special votes of thanks were given to Mr Smith, who had been on the board of 'Colthrop Board & Paper Mills Ltd' since the First World War and had 'thrown himself single-mindedly into the task of building the company up', to where it was.

However, the company was on the eve of change. Mr 'Jack' Henry (son of John Henry, who had made the paper mill a success) died in 1950. Two sons of Samuel Cropper died in the same period, Mr Shirley Cropper in 1947 (leaving an estate of over £60,000), and Mr Digby Cropper in 1953, who had 'served the company faithfully for over fifty years'.

Memories of Life at Colthrop

Among the good folk to live and work at Colthrop was Mrs Kath Huttings (née Muttram), who now lives in The Hollands but who was born and bred at Colthrop village. She was one of the ten children (four sons and six daughters) of George and Alice Muttram, who came to Colthrop from Devon just

Colthrop Mill's Fire Brigade photographed in front of the pay office with their Leyland fire engine in 1938. Left to right, back row: *Fred Hayward, Bill Muttram, Len Breach, David 'Jock' Gibson, George Muttram, Nelson Turner, Fred Berry;* front row: *Arthur 'Digger' Blissett, Wilf Canning, Mr J.M. Henry, Bill Patterson (chief fire officer), Cyril Muttram and Jim Berry.*

before the First World War.

George Muttram moved to Thatcham from Plymouth in 1911, following a fire at the Lee Mill Bridge paper mill in Ivybridge (which had been acquired by the Henry brothers in 1908). The paper machine from that mill was later relocated to Colthrop and Mr Muttram came too – living in Thatcham and helping to install the machine at the mill, prior to taking up residence at No.12, Colthrop Cottages with his family.

The Muttrams already had three children and seven more were later born at Colthrop – they were William (Bill), Wilfred, Alfred, Cyril, Dora, Beryl, Ethel, Kathleen, Violet and Joan. Mr Muttram was employed as a maintenance fitter at the mill, doing jobs like sharpening blades for the cutting machinery in the chopping house. He also became an auxiliary fireman when the mill fire brigade was set up after the war.

Colthrop Mill's auxiliary firemen were full-time mill employees who were on call to fight any fires that might break out. In their cottages beside the canal were bells which could be rung in an emergency to summon them to the mill fire station, where Colthrop's fire engine was kept. As a girl, Kath Muttram recalls taking dinner – inside two plates, one on top of the other – to her father on night duty at the fire station.

Born in 1920, Kath Muttram as she then was has fond memories of Colthrop village. The small community was 'a very friendly place' and the folk who lived there were 'very close' – everyone helped everyone else. The children played together and became good swimmers at a young age – 'we all fell in the river at some time and so learned the hard way!' Whenever there was a wedding, everyone got invited to it.

When the family grew larger the Muttrams moved

Colthrop Cottages, beside the canal, early in the twentieth century. One of the cottages housed a small shop to serve the needs of the hamlet community.

from No.12 to No.18, Colthrop Cottages. The houses then had no gas or electricity but were lit by paraffin lamps. Fuel was obtained from the mill, using a 'chitty' which was taken to the paraffin shed. House No.20 was the local shop, established by its tenants Mr and Mrs Nightingale (it operated as such until the mill canteen was opened in the 1950s).

Several tradesmen also served the little community at Colthrop, including Wyatt's butcher, Jeffries' baker and Pinnock's coalman. Mrs Hutchings especially recalls milkman Harry Pickett, who lived at house No.2, which had a dairy alongside. His three cows supplied milk, which he delivered around the cottages by horse and cart, filling the cans which the residents kept for this purpose just inside their front doors.

Also adjoining No.2 was the Reading Room which served as a general function room and the Sunday school. This was run by Miss Evelyn Henry (daughter of mill owner Mr John Maclean Henry) and catered for about two dozen children who lived in the cottages. Miss Henry taught religious education to the children of the Muttram, Canning, Turner, Ralph, Denness, Berry, Maisey and Nightingale families here.

For the children the highlight of the year was the annual August day trip to the Henry family summer home, a bungalow at Felpham near Bognor. In the care of the daughters of the Henry family – Louise Elizabeth (Betty), Nora, Ruth and Evelyn – the trip to Sussex was made by hired coach. An enjoyable day was had by all and the children were given currant buns and bananas as they set off on the journey home.

When she left school at the age of 14, Kath went into service with the Henry family at The Gables (since demolished, the house stood where Panasonic is based today). She worked as 'between maid', serving and clearing away meals and cleaning the bedrooms. Mr J.M. Henry is remembered as 'a real gentleman' and Mrs Nora Henry as 'very strict', using a white handkerchief to check the quality of the dusting.

Kath Muttram, seen among the inhabitants of Colthrop, celebrating VE-Day in 1945. Left to right, back row: *Bill Muttram, David Turner, Lilly Gregory, Maisy Richardson, Dolly Denness, Pearl Turner, Mabel Turner, Barbara Turner, Winifred Muttram, Mrs Smart, Marion Pickett, Mrs Miles, Joan Muttram, Kath Muttram, Jean Braidwood, ?, Dorothy Braidwood, Violet Muttram, Fred Smart, Tom Blissett;* middle row: *Mrs Muttram, Mrs Maisey, Mrs Hatward, Mrs Turner, Mrs Tanner, Mrs Cannings, Kate Taylor, ?, Joan Richardson, Joyce Turner, Beatrice Swan, John Braidwood, Minnie Breach, Geoff Tanner, Len Breach, Mr Muttram, Mrs Breach;* front row: *Ron Tanner, Jean Breach, ?, ?, Pam Smart, Sybil Pickett, Barbara Chivers, Maureen Smart, Joyce Muttram, Roy Miles, Daphne Alder, Keith Smart, Grace Breach, Brian Miles, Raymond Breach.*

There was also a cook and a young girl who worked as a kitchen maid, along with a cowman (Mr Baldwin) and a gardener (Mr Hutchings – no relation). Although she lived just across the fields, Kath had to live in and was only allowed home on alternate Sunday mornings and afternoons. Her day started at 6.30a.m., cleaning fireplaces and lighting fires, and went on until late. For all this her pay was a mere £1 a month.

In 1945 Kath married Charles Hutchings. He served in the Royal Navy until 1948 whereupon he obtained employment at Colthrop Mill as a maintenance finer. Kath's brothers all worked at the mill too: the eldest, William, was employed as a chargehand in the board mill; Alfred worked on the Ivybridge machine; Cyril was a carpenter and Wilfred became personnel officer at Colthrop Mill when he left the Navy.

Whilst Kath and her husband moved into Thatcham in 1947, her parents stayed on at No.18 Colthrop Cottages. Her father died in 1949 but her mother continued to live at the cottage with her unmarried sister, Violet, until 1957. Kath recalls her time at Colthrop with affection and – based on her family's involvement with Colthrop Mill through two generations – thinks that, all in all, it was 'not a bad firm to work for'.

The Rise and Fall of Reeds (Colthrop)

By the mid-1950s, 'Colthrop Board & Paper Mills' had been established as such for over 30 years but was about to take on a new identity. Few of the individuals who had helped to establish the concern, such as members of the Henry and Cropper families, were still involved in running it, although John Henry's grandson – John Richard Henry – was managing director.

Born in 1910 at The Gables, home of his late father Mr J.M. Henry, this John Henry presented long-service awards to Colthrop employees at the first formal occasion on which this was done in 1956. The mill's workers had a tradition of long service and 16 of them at this event had, between them, put in 780 years' service – an average of almost half-a-century for every man present. In 1956 the mill employed approximately 900 people.

Mr Henry spoke of the 'wonderful record of long and loyal service' these men had achieved and tried to picture what Colthrop was like 50 years earlier. Then, the board mill did not exist but three machines were involved in paper manufacture. 'Everything came to the mills by canal except for one horse and van' – it went to Reading with a load of new paper and returned with waste.

Most employees were male but about 30 girls were employed in the bag room. The mill had two water wheels for driving the beaters (pulping machines)

Mr A.J. Prouting, a stoker, receives a retirement clock from Mr Roy Haines, transport manager, after 57 years' service at Colthrop Mill.

Fitter's labourer Mr C. Read is presented with a clock by Mr B.D. Cowell, chief engineer, on his retirement after 23 years at Colthrop Mill.

along with steam boilers and a gas plant. 'The mills have changed their appearance by having a fire now and again', Mr Henry said, perhaps in something of an understatement: 'There have been six or seven biggish fires'.

The recipients of the awards offered thanks. Mr W. Lane said: 'I am sure we shall all prize these presents which will remind us of the happy days we have spent at Colthrop'. Mr W. Liddiard said: 'We used to work 72 hours a week. All the holidays we had were three days a year – Easter, Whit Mondays and August bank holidays'. Moreover, 'We always worked on Christmas Day'.

Another veteran volunteered: 'I used to walk to and from Newbury every day, and I have never felt so well since we have come by bus!'. In the postwar years, a regular bus service ran between Newbury and Colthrop, coinciding with shift changes at the mill, and was well patronised. Also, by 1952 up to 400 cyclists travelled to and fro daily between Thatcham and Colthrop Mill.

However, as things had changed in the past, they were about to change again. Mr J.R. Henry himself left the mill in 1958 (he died in 1993 at the age of 82).

The view looking north-west from the Power Station in 1958 towards the village of Thatcham.

Pictured in front of the new North Mill board machine are VIPs, left to right: Mr Hector Paul and Mr Cyril Oliver (directors of A.E. Reed & Co.), Mr Stanley Barrow (superintendent of North and South Mills), Mr John Henry (Colthrop managing director), ?.

The Power Station at the North Mill viewed from the west soon after completion in 1958.

A view of the new North Mill at Colthrop, from an original oil painting presented to the Mill management by Taylor Woodrow, the main building contractors.

The No. 3 board machine installed at the North Mill in 1958 – it had many advanced features.

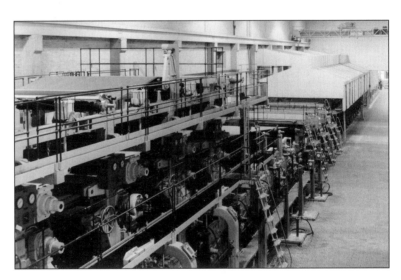

The view looking east from the Power Station across storage tanks to Colthrop railway crossing.

Sometime prior to this, the successful paper and board company at Colthrop had invited another business – that of Albert E. Reed (Aylesford, Kent) – to become shareholders. In fact, the Reed Group acquired Colthrop in 1958!

Even before the takeover, the Reed and Colthrop managements were jointly involved in plans to extend the complex. In 1950, Containers had relocated to a new site north of the railway line – the original site south of the railway line was becoming congested. From 1953, plans were underway to add a brand new (North) Board Mill here to the existing (South) paper and board mills.

The North Board Mill was built by Taylor Woodrow Construction Ltd, who started work on it in May 1955. On a 40-acre site, a huge self-contained mill – a thousand feet long – was erected, with storage facilities, workshops and other facilities. At the same time, Holst & Co. Ltd began work on building a separate coal-fired power station, with a turbine to drive the mill's machinery.

Inside the mill, a new board machine was erected jointly by Walmsley's (Bury) Ltd and Walker Brothers (Wigan) Ltd, mainly to manufacture folding box board. The North Board Mill was built at a cost of £5,000,000 and was one of the world's most advanced mills. It was the first new mill to be built in Britain

for a quarter of a century, commencing production on 13 January 1958.

By this date, there were actually four separate Reed Group companies operating at Colthrop on a 160-acre complex, which employed over 2,000 people. From this time on, however, a decline set in and finally the mill's two paper machines were shut down, one in 1966 and the other in 1971. Only cardboard was made at Colthrop thereafter – after nearly 230 years, it no longer made paper.

In 1980, Colthrop's three machines produced 114,000 tons of cardboard but the South Mill was closed in 1985. Demolition started the following year, with its 160 feet high chimney coming down brick-by-brick (Thatcham lost one of its best-known landmarks), and this was completed in November 1988. In that year too, Reed International sold all of its manufacturing interests at Colthrop.

Over the next few years, several convoluted changes of ownership took place but nothing could stem the decline. In 1991, Colthrop's North Board Mill employed only 240 people but still produced some 60,000 tonnes of cardboard. After little more than four decades, the North Board Mill closed on 31 July 2000, being demolished in the winter of 2001/2. This final act really was the end of an era.

Workaday Memories of Colthrop's South Mill

Many people who worked at Colthrop still live locally in retirement, and one such person is Mr Bert Harfitt, who worked at the mill in two stints totalling 23 years. Born in 1922, Bert grew up in Portsmouth, where he completed an engineering apprenticeship but his family were bombed out in 1941 and evacuated to Newbury. Then, he joined the RAF as an engine fitter but upon being demobbed after the war he went to work at Colthrop Mill in 1946. At that date there was no North Board Mill, so he was employed as a maintenance fitter in the South Mill.

Bert still has his first pay slip for January 1947, when he was paid 2s.6d. an hour – he earned £6 or so for a basic week of 48 hours plus overtime. At that time, the mill employed about 1000 people and worked around the clock on a shift system. These workers travelled in from a wide area, on bicycles, by bus and (to a lesser extent) by car.

Newbury & District Motor Services ran a frequent service from the town to Colthrop Mill, with runs timed to coincide with three shift changes. The first bus left Newbury at 5.30a.m. but Bert recalls travelling on the 7.00a.m. bus, which arrived in time for the day shift starting at 7.30a.m. – the buses stopped just over the railway level crossing outside the South Mill time office.

Colthrop Mill then produced both paper and board using two machines, the second of which was fairly

An aerial view of the new North Mill from the east in 1958 – the Power Station is in the foreground and a footbridge across the railway (left) connects it to the South Mill.

The South Mill at Colthrop where Bert Harfitt worked, seen from the North Mill Power Station.

The view west from the Power Station, with Fields factory (left) and the new North Mill (right).

Bert Harfitt engaged in board production at the South Mill in its last year of production, 1985.

new, having only been installed in 1939. The two machines were run 24 hours a day, six days a week. For routine maintenance purposes, the machines were shut down from 6.00a.m. Sunday to 6.00a.m. Monday each week (and for a week at a time in summer and at Christmas).

Bert Harfitt and Don Read, his fitter's mate, were part of a team of fitters who worked in pairs for six weeks at a time on alternate 12-hour day and night shifts, dealing immediately with any breakdown of either machine. Otherwise, the fitters all worked 'normal days' maintaining the two machines – including the regular Sundays, for which overtime was paid.

Later, the North Board Mill was built across the railway line and Bert recalls seeing the huge new buildings being erected between 1955 and 1958. The North Board Mill began operation in January of the latter year but Bert continued to work at the South Mill – the two mills were treated as two separate entities, with their own maintenance teams, unless extra hands were required in an emergency.

Bert recalls that many Colthrop employees in this period had long histories of working there and many worked well beyond normal retirement age. One colleague he remembers well was Mr R. 'Dickie' Buckland, who retired on 30 April 1958, after 41 years' service as a labourer at the age of 87 years. On the same date, Mr Frederick Richardson retired, aged 78, with a remarkable record of 61 years continuous service as a chopping house attendant, having started work at Colthrop Mill in 1897 – during the Victorian era!

Bert Harfitt himself left the mill in 1960 to work as an insurance salesman, although he came back to Colthrop's South Mill in 1975, doing shift work on board production. (No paper was made at Colthrop after 1971.) By this time, his pay slips show that his wages were £1.17p an hour and wages were now paid in a sealed brown envelopes rather than the reusable round tins customarily used by the pay office in earlier days.

Colthrop's two machines now produced cardboard, using mostly waste paper but some wood pulp. These raw materials underwent beating and refining treatment prior to being introduced to the 'wet' end of the machine where the sheets are formed. Each of Colthrop's machines was 350 feet long and picked up fibres from seven vats along its length to build up the board in layers before it reached the 'dry' end as a finished product.

This was the work in which Bert was involved from 1975 but in 10 years it was all over. Foreign competition meant that Colthrop's two board machines were becoming uneconomic – each was shut down now and again, initially for days but later for weeks at a time. Eventually, the workforce was put on a 3-day week and finally given notice of redundancy in February 1985.

Bert's last pay slips show that he was being paid £2.77 an hour and working 51 hours a week. On 14 May 1985, the South Mill closed down for good: it was demolished a couple of years later. Aged 63 and close to retirement, Bert accepted the redundancy package then offered to employees. They received a month's pay for each year of service at the mill, plus a year's holiday money. He still has fond memories of his working days at Colthrop's South Mill.

Chapter IX

River, Rail and Canal

The Smiths of Chamberhouse Mill

Today, Chamberhouse Mill is yet another of Thatcham's residential developments but for some six centuries it was a working grist (corn) mill. From the late-fourteenth century onwards, the medieval inhabitants of the locality took their corn here to be ground into flour, a task for which the waters of the River Kennet provided a free power supply.

The mill then formed a part of the Crookham estate, being leased by the lords of the manor to tenant-millers, most of whose names have been lost to us. The first recorded name of a miller appears in a will of 1656, made by Dowse Fuller, one of the estate owners, who left a bequest to 'Thomas Eastman, his miller at Chamberhouse'.

In the second quarter of the nineteenth century Charles Witherington was the miller at Chamberhouse, and in the third quarter it was Phillip Watts. However, in 1882 the Smith family became the tenant-millers and remained so for the next eight decades, right up to the time when the mill finally ceased production and was shut down.

The first member of the family to hold the lease of Chamberhouse Mill was Henry Smith, born in 1841. He was born into an extended family of millers, of which branches were connected with other working Berkshire mills at Mapledurham, Tidmarsh, Padworth and Brimpton. By this period, the Tulls were lords of the manor of Crookham.

Family tradition has it that Henry was born at Brimpton Mill (although the Census records his birthplace as Bradfield). Aged 41, he came to work the mill – and live in the spacious millhouse – at Chamberhouse with his wife Sophia (born at Beaconsfield in 1839) and their growing family, at that date consisting of one daughter and three Sons.

The daughter was Anne Louise (born 1866 in Reading); the sons were Alfred (born 1870), Henry (born 1874) and Frederick (born 1877). All been born at Brimpton Mill – the two older boys were already working as millers with their father. There were two more daughters, Lillian and Mabel Jane (born in 1883 at Chamberhouse Mill).

In 1887, after Henry Smith had been the tenant for five years, 'Squire' Tull the landlord decided to install new machinery at the mill. The millwrights firm of Messrs Armsfield of Ringwood, Hampshire, undertook the work. The contract took several months to complete, with much of the new equipment arriving by rail from suppliers.

A pair of 18 cwt grindstones were fitted, along with replacement backboards, floats, iron shafts and drawing tackle – to power this machinery, new water-wheels were erected. In a later indenture, the whole is described as a 'Water Corn Mill ... with all and singular the wheels, mill gear, running tackle, machinery, implements and fittings' and so on.

Beyond the mill itself, the same indenture records that the Smith family held the 'dwelling house', woodhouse, cowhouse, pigsties, stabling, carthouse, four cottages and other buildings. In all, they had use of a total of 16 acres, 1 rood and 21 perches of land, including yards, garden, meadow and 'the use of the waters' belonging to the mill.

The family became very popular in the neighbourhood as the years passed. Henry Smith took an active part in the parish assembly of 1894 (proposing a candidate who was elected to Thatcham's new Parish Council), although he never sought election as a councillor for himself. He is recalled as a kindly soul whose interests lay elsewhere.

He was fond of animals and kept cattle and pigs at Chamberhouse Mill – there is a tradition that if one of his animals was ill he would return from his local (the Swan, just over the railway crossing) with 'medicinal' sherry for it! He was equally fond of the wildlife at the mill, especially the dabchicks which nested on the Kennet.

As the years passed, Henry Smith's children grew up. Some moved out of the millhouse. Daughters Annie and Mabel Jane married into farming families, the former into that of Bucknell at Aldermaston and the latter into that of Laye at Thatcham. Son Fred married into the Brooks family, the well-known Thatcham corn merchants.

One son and daughter – Sidney and Lillian – never married and stayed on at the millhouse in adulthood.

A distant view of Chamberhouse Mill in summer, looking downstream along the River Kennet.

The rural setting of Chamberhouse Mill is evident in this postcard view, with swans on the River Kennet sometime around the turn of the century.

Spot the difference! New trees for old – seen from almost the same vantage point near Chamberhouse Mill, older trees have been felled and new ones planted alongside the river.

Their mother Sophia died in August 1903, aged 64, and was buried in Thatcham cemetery – from this time, they helped to run the home as well as the mill. Brother Fred lived with his wife at Oxford Lodge in Station Road.

On the morning of Sunday 9 May 1909, Sidney and Lillian set off from Chamberhouse to attend morning service at St Mary's Church, meeting Fred and his wife on the way. Alone at the mill, their father, aged 68 and suffering with a bad leg, tragically fell into the river and drowned. He was buried with his late wife at the cemetery.

After Henry Smith died in 1909, his family continued to run a milling business at Chamberhouse, and still traded under the name of 'Henry Smith & Sons'. Sidney stayed on at the millhouse with his sister Lillian, both unmarried, and shared the management of the mill with brother Fred who lived with his wife in Station Road, Thatcham.

The brothers had been granted a nine year lease on Chamberhouse Mill by their landlord, 'Squire' A.R. Tull of Crookham House. Signed on 8 April 1909, it made the pair joint tenants in charge of the mill and confirmed their rights and responsibilities there,

including 'all game, wildfowl, rabbits and fish', along with hunting and fishing rights.

The brothers employed six men at the mill. Fred was in charge of the day-to-day running of the mill business. He was recalled by mill employees as a punctual boss – 'You could set your clock by the moment Mr Fred came into the mill of a morning', one of them claimed. Sidney supervised technical aspects of flour production at the mill.

Chamberhouse flour was made from a mixture of English and Canadian wheat. The former was obtained from local farmers and the latter imported via Avonmouth docks. During the First World War when imported wheat was scarce, Sidney Smith's solution was to mix barley, bean meal and maize meal with the flour to keep up production.

After the War the Smiths found themselves with a new landlord. Mr A.S.B. Tull succeeded his father and entered into new tenancy arrangements with the family. By an agreement dated 14 May 1920, Sidney and Fred Smith were obliged to accept annual leases on Chamberhouse Mill and they lost their fishing rights, which passed to Mr Tull.

It is said that the brothers heaved sacks of flour about as well as any of their employees, earning the respect of the men because they never expected them to do anything they couldn't do too! Two mill employees lived with their families in a pair of cottages down the road from the mill, one of them being the mill's carters, the Hiscock family.

Ted Hiscock was the Chamberhouse Mill carter for many years. The cart was maintained in fine condition and was pulled by 'two of the finest horses' ever seen, another employee remembered. If they came to a hill – even with a heavy load – 'they used to take it at full gallop'. The horses were shod by George Pike, the Thatcham blacksmith.

In all, the mill owned four horses, the other two being used to pull its delivery van. This was in the charge of Harry Marshall (whose family lived in the other cottage). Deliveries of flour and pig food were made over a wide area, taking half a day to Bradfield and a whole day to Chieveley – Chamberhouse flour cost a guinea per 280 lb sack.

In the millhouse, sister Lillian looked after the domestic side of things, assisted by a housemaid. Working together in the dairy, they made quantities of delicious golden butter that was famed for miles around. The millhouse larder was also stocked with eggs and milk produced by the chickens and cows, which were kept in the mill's meadow.

Chamberhouse Mill was the venue for a number of local gatherings between the wars, not least the church fêtes held in its attractive garden. In the summer months too, family and friends enjoyed swimming and boating here, with delicious teas laid on by Miss Lillian, who served up homemade gingerbread, scones, butter and strawberry jam.

However, as the years passed, time began to take

The River Kennet is seen here in full flow as it approaches Chamberhouse, at a time when it was very much a working mill run by the Smith family – the mill race leads off to the right.

An idyllic view of Chamberhouse Mill seen here in 1908 – corn was milled at Chamberhouse for almost 600 years, until 1965.

its toll. Over in Thatcham, at Oxford Lodge, Fred Smith's wife, Nellie, died in February 1934, aged 50. Their daughter Freda stayed on at the family home to look after her father. Then, on 22 November 1936, Sidney Smith died aged 61, leaving his sister Lillian living alone at the mill.

Widower Fred and his grown-up daughter thereupon moved into Chamberhouse Mill and Lillian, making way for Freda, the new housekeeper, moved out. (Miss Lillian Smith never married and lived to a good age; she died in March, 1959, aged 80 years. Her married sister Mabel Jane (Lay) died on 30 August 1980, at the ripe old age of 98 years.°

In 1939, soon after the Second World War broke out, the Crookham estate was sold by Mr Tull and so Chamberhouse Mill had a new landlord – Mr John Henry, of Colthrop Mill. As tenant, Fred Smith managed to keep the mill in production right up to his death on 21 January 1965, at the age of 89 years. At that, the mill machinery fell silent!

Chamberhouse Mill had made its last flour and now lay empty for a few years. At last, Mr J.R. Henry

sold the premises to John Bennet (Properties) Ltd. In turn, it was purchased by property developer Mr M.V. Raphael, who demolished the millhouse, converted the mill and – along with new construction – built 11 homes on the site in the very early 1970s.

Life on the Lines

The railway came to Thatcham when the GWR opened what was initially a long branch line from their main line at Reading to Hungerford on 21 December 1847. At Thatcham, the railway station lay a mile to the south of the village on the Crookham Road (which became Station Road after the railway arrived). The station was built on the site of three cottages 'conveniently' destroyed by fire about in 1844.

Like others on the line, Thatcham's original station was a timber construction – a 'wooden shanty' – offering deficient accommodation. The down (Newbury) platform was so exposed that passengers waiting for trains got saturated when it rained and there was no ladies' waiting room at the station. No goods shed was built at the station until 1850, moreover, as goods traffic did not begin on the line until a year after it opened.

From this primitive station, the people of Thatcham began and ended their railway journeys, being treated to a 'sulphurous' ride along the Kennet Valley. For the first 27 years of its life, the Kennet Valley line, in common with other GWR tracks, was broad gauge, unlike other railway companies.

However, because of the problems caused by the difference in the size of the gauge, the GWR eventually converted its tracks to standard gauge – the Kennet Valley line was converted in the space of a week in 1874. The line was gradually extended beyond Hungerford so that it became the GWR main

The station looking west, seen from the end of the up platform in around 1920. Mr Leslie White waits for a London-bound train on his way to Australia! (He was emigrating).

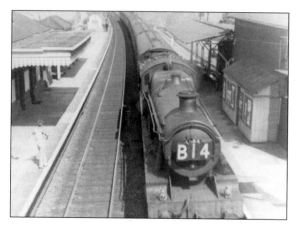

The station looking east, seen from the old footbridge in around 1960, with a steam hauled stopping train at the down (Newbury bound) platform.

The station viewed from the old footbridge, with a semaphore signal in the foreground. Among the station buildings at this time there was a goods shed behind the down platform (right).

Another view of the station as it was in the early 1960s, looking west from the end of the down platform. The long-gone goods shed (now a car park) is clearly visible on the left.

Thatcham Station looking east past the up side station building in the 1960s – an express train for the West Country can be seen passing through, hauled by a 'Warship' class diesel.

Viewed from the road, Thatcham's original station footbridge (erected 1908) can be seen behind the old style level-crossing gates – this bridge was demolished in 1965.

A Newbury-bound diesel stopping train departs from Thatcham Station (looking west) in 1985 during the interim period between old and new station buildings.

Another view of the station looking east in the 1960s. Here, a diesel multiple unit forms a west bound stopping train, as steam hauled trains are replaced by new motive power!

Thatcham's Last Stationmaster

Not everybody looks back on their working days with fondness, but railwaymen often used to. One railwayman who did so was the late Mr Harold Thomas Grinham. He was a railwayman for 42 years, the last 17 of them as stationmaster at Thatcham's old railway station. In his retirement, he was able to look back on his working days in this role as something special, since – as things turned out – they were the last 17 years of Thatcham as a fully staffed railway station too.

Born at Cholsey, Mr Grinham joined the service of the Great Western Railway in 1922, and worked first at Paddington and then at Maidenhead and Henley, before becoming a relief stationmaster. From 1944 he was stationmaster at Midgham and then in 1949 – shortly after the railways were nationalised – he came to Thatcham in the same capacity. Here, he lived with his family at No.4 Station Road where he was to spend the rest of his life, both in work and in retirement.

In the early days of British Railways, there were 23 staff under the control of the stationmaster at Thatcham. One of these staff was responsible for opening up the station in time for the first stopping train of the day, around 6.45a.m., and another would close up each evening after the last train had called at about 10.30p.m. At this time there were a dozen or so stopping trains in each direction every weekday – then (as now), Thatcham was relatively well served by rail.

As stationmaster, Mr Grinham did not have to arrive for duty until about 7.45a.m. and he would normally finish work about 5.30p.m. During the working day, it was his responsibility to ensure that all the employees around the station carried out their particular duties, although the day-to-day routine

line to the West Country from 1906. The 'Cornish Riviera Express' first came through Thatcham in July of that year.

Complaints about Thatcham's station finally resulted in it being rebuilt. Messrs Goodchilds of Reading undertook the work – timber gave way to masonry as improved accommodation was erected for both staff and passengers. The new station buildings were opened on 24 August 1893 – the staff at this time consisted of a stationmaster, parcel porter, goods porter, two boy porters and two crossing keepers.

When the railways were nationalised in 1948, the GWR became the Western Region of British Railways. That year a new stationmaster, Harold Grinham, came to Thatcham – he was to be the last! He had a staff of 23 under him and some 120 trains a day passed through the station, of which number a dozen in each direction stopped here.

However, under the Beeching Plan of 1963, Thatcham's station – like most others on the Kennet Valley line – became unstaffed and the station buildings were demolished in November 1965.

The footbridge was also dismantled and lifting barriers replaced the old level crossing gates. Thatcham's signal box was demolished in May 1978. However, the train service continued to be well patronised and British Rail decided to build a new station at Thatcham.

Construction began early in 1987 and progressed rapidly. By the summer the work had been completed, at a cost of £177,000. Mayor of Thatcham, Mr Mike Rees, officially opened the new station on 8 August of that year and £500 of special low-price tickets were sold in just two hours. Local commuters travelled on the last locomotive hauled train on the Kennet Valley line on 3 July 1992. Thatcham is once again served by the trains of a privatised railway company today.

A track level view, looking east showing the station buildings erected at Thatcham in 1893 and demolished in 1965 – this was the station of which Harold Grinham had charge.

On the occasion of the opening of the town's new station buildings on 8 August 1987, the man who then took charge – senior railman Mr Norman Collins – shook hands with Thatcham Mayor Mike Rees (seen here with his wife Janet).

was left to them. Some of these employees came in from Newbury and elsewhere, but some were Thatcham people and well-known characters in the village at that time.

Among the employees under Mr Grinham were nine signalmen, one for each of the three local signalboxes – Thatcham Station, Colthrop Mills and the Ordnance Depot. At the latter two places there were also railway offices to deal with traffic in and out, each under the charge of a foreman: Reg Wise was in charge at Colthrop and Ernie Ayres at the Depot. Of the nine signalmen, the best known was Frank Mayow, who worked in the Thatcham Station signal box.

Frank Mayow had begun his railway service with the GWR at Oxford in May 1898, and came to Thatcham as a signalman in 1903. He worked in this capacity for literally half a century – before the First World War, he used to ring a bell from the signal box window to let intending passengers know their train was approaching. It had also been rung as a Greenwich time signal at 10a.m. every morning – in Harold Grinham's time, this bell was still in the stationmaster's office.

Thatcham Station itself was then a hive of activity. In between the passenger trains there was much freight traffic to deal with, such as coal and waste

paper for Colthrop Mills. One freight train would arrive in the morning from Reading and its locomotive would remain all day at Thatcham to shunt wagons from later trains. It was not at all unusual to have three freight trains, totalling 150 wagons, stabled at Theale, Reading and Didcot, all heading for Colthrop sidings.

Some of the coal was destined for local coal merchant Eddie Pinnock, whose son – Tom – would come down to the station with a lorry to take loads back to their Broadway yard. During the morning too, the local 'carrier', Les Barker, would arrive to pick up and deliver parcels from the goods shed then located at the station, which had a 2-ton crane to transship loads. By the 1950s, the freight tonnage handled at Thatcham Station worked out at a six figure total in a year.

At this time Colthrop Mill was being expanded (with the building of the North Mill) and Greenham air-base was being revamped by the American Airforce, bringing considerable volumes of traffic to Thatcham Station – over the course of three to four months, some 600–800 tons of cement were offloaded here every week. In terms of train movements, something like 120 trains passed through Thatcham, with or without stopping, in the course of the average day.

Thatcham Station staff outside the goods shed in 1949. Left to right, back row: ?, Archie Mann, Albert Arnold, Margaret Miles, ?, Frank Ashfield, Alt Myers, Ernie Ayres; front row: 'Billie' Draper, W.J. Elsey, Elsie French, Harold Grinham (stationmaster), Pat Wise.

Stationmaster Harold Grinham being presented with a clock on the occasion of his retirement from railway service in 1965.

Looking west from the window of Thatcham's signal box in 1972, a pair of Brush Type 2 diesel locomotives haul their freight train from the depot sidings onto the main line.

Thatcham's signal box, opened in 1921 and demolished in 1978 – it replaced an earlier box that stood opposite, where signalman Frank Mayow worked from 1903. In this view of May 1971, signalman P.B. Kelly inspects flooding caused by a summer cloudburst.

Amidst the stopping passenger and freight trains, through expresses – such as the 'Cornish Riviera' and the 'Torbay Express' – would need a clear run through Thatcham Station on their way to and from the West Country. Later in the day, commuters would return from London and Reading by stopping train before the activity subsided with the departure of the last local train of the day. In those days, passenger trains even ran on Christmas Day and Boxing Day.

However, by the 1960s all was not well on the railways and in 1965 Thatcham's old station lost its staff and was demolished. Mr Grinham retired from railway service but lived long enough to see the new Thatcham Station opened in August, 1987. He observed that the station as he knew it bore 'no comparison with today', for the present Thatcham Station is but a shadow of its former self. Sadly, Harold Grinham – Thatcham's last stationmaster – died in April 1988.

Fall and Rise of the Navigation

The River Kennet through Thatcham was made navigable when the Kennet Navigation opened from the River Thames at Reading as far as Newbury in 1723. This waterway was extended through to Bath and Bristol with the creation of the Kennet and Avon

Canal, which opened in 1810. From this date the canal became a major cross-country route and carried a considerable volume of traffic.

However, the Kennet and Avon Canal's prosperity was short-lived. In 1841 the Great Western Railway was opened between London and Bristol in direct competition with the waterway. On the canals, ice in winter and drought in summer caused delays to traffic, occasionally for weeks at a time.

Even under the most favourable conditions, goods in barges took at least three days to reach London from Bristol whereas the railway brought them up in

Looking east on the canal towpath in about 1908 – note the station goods shed (right) *and the Swan Inn* (left) *in the distance.*

Grace White sitting next to Widmead Lock on the Kennet and Avon Canal on a summer's afternoon in days gone by. After years of dereliction, the canal was restored and fully reopened in 1990.

113

The road from Thatcham to the south crossed the Kennet and Avon Canal on an old timber bridge in days gone by – seen here from the canal towpath and looking south-east.

Kennet and Avon Canal looking east from Monkey Marsh Lock towards Thatcham Station in about 1914.

The view north across the old Chamberhouse Lane swingbridge (since replaced) prior to the canal's restoration in 1988.

The view, looking west into Monkey Marsh Lock, seen here in derelict condition in 1988.

Left: *The view, looking west into Monkey Marsh Lock, seen here in restored condition in 1993.*

Below left: *Children playing on the almost dry bed of the derelict canal at Chamberhouse Lane swingbridge in the mid-1980s.*

Below right: *A family group by the top gate of the derelict Monkey Marsh Lock on the canal (looking east) in the mid-1980s.*

The first boat to enter Monkey Marsh Lock in over 40 years, seen here in July 1990 from which date the entire canal became navigable again.

just three hours! On the canal a decline set in as traffic and receipts plummeted and in 1852 the Kennet and Avon sold out to the GWR.

The railway company made a loss on the canal in 1877 and the deficit increased year by year thereafter. In the twentieth century the GWR (and later the Railway Executive) tried to close the canal completely on a number of occasions but faced fierce opposition from local people.

Up until the First World War there was still some regular long distance traffic on the canal. Coal from the Midlands still came up as far as Newbury. Canal carrier Jack Garner had a regular trip from Colthrop Mill to Bristol with cargoes of paper, sugar bags, wrappers and other paper products.

In 1949 a local branch of the Inland Waterways Association was established to fight to keep the canal open. In February 1949, the British Transport Commission took control of the Kennet and Avon Canal – although still navigable it was in poor repair and its future was uncertain.

By 1951 the condition of the canal had deteriorated further and was no longer open throughout – several sections had become unusable through lack of maintenance. John Gould, a Newbury canal carrier, initiated High Court action against the British Transport Commission to try and keep the waterway open.

The Kennet and Avon Canal Trust was formed to preserve the waterway in June 1962, and the following year entered into a 'constructive co-operation' with the new canal administration, the British Waterways Board. In reopening the canal throughout, a huge task lay ahead of them.

For example, of the eight locks between Newbury and Reading, two brick-built ones needed some work and two more needed adapting, but four of the original Kennet Navigation turf-sided locks required complete re-builds – their total restoration costs were estimated at £300,000.

Thatcham's Monkey Marsh lock was one of the last to be rebuilt before the canal could be reopened throughout its length. Restoration work on the old turf-sided lock at Monkey Marsh began in June 1989, funded by local councils, British Waterways and the Kennet and Avon Canal Trust.

It was completed the following summer and opened at a special ceremony on 17 July 1990. Mr Tony Wiseman (Chairman of Berkshire County Council) unveiled a plaque and a crowd of 200 onlookers cheered as the first boat passed through the lock for some 40 years.

The canal was officially reopened throughout its length by the Queen at Devizes on 8 August 1990. Boats are again a regular sight on the waterway through Thatcham, although the Kennet and Avon Canal is today used by leisure rather than commercial craft, as it was in times past.

Chapter X

Car, Bus and Lorry

The Bath Road Through Thatcham

Travellers from London to Bristol have passed through Thatcham for centuries but the Great Bath Road was really an eighteenth century creation which came into being with the growth of Bath as a spa town. The road was little more than a track until the stagecoach age, which resulted in the building of turnpike roads – there was a turnpike gate at the Garden Centre roundabout until 1878.

When the railways forced the stagecoaches off the roads, the turnpikes went into decline until the late - nineteenth century. However, there was a revival in road travel with the coming of bicycles and motorcars from that time. In 1888 Berkshire County Council was established and quickly assumed responsibility for road maintenance.

By November, 1890, the Bath Road through Thatcham was reported to be 'in the hands of the County Council and a strong staff of road-men employed'. By January the following year we learn that the roadmen were 'mending our roads in the village with granite.' Before the end of 1894 the Bath Road through Thatcham had been re-metalled with Cranmore stone instead of ordinary gravel.

However, there was a tendency for motorcars' pneumatic tyres to suck the binding material out of the road surface, so that in dry weather especially, passing vehicles raised clouds of dust, and roads required frequent repairs at ratepayers' expense. This was the case in Thatcham, where the Parish Council discussed the provision of a water cart as a solution in 1897. Having sprinklers across the back, these carts had been used on the roads in earlier days to keep down the dust, but they could not cope in the new circumstances. The Parish Council decided that such a measure 'was not considered feasible at present' anyway!

In April, 1900, the Automobile Club (precursor of the RAC) organised a 1,000-mile Round Britain Rally. Starting from London at 7.00a.m. on 23 April, more than 80 entrants, in a variety of vehicles, stopped in Reading for breakfast at mid-morning. Then they drove on along the Bath Road – passing groups of fascinated villagers in Thatcham – reaching Bristol that evening.

Whilst some of the cars were capable of doing up to 40mph, there was then a national speed limit of just 12mph. Policemen stood at milestones along the Bath Road recording the numbers and times of the passing vehicles, but no action was taken although some cars did break the speed limit. The dry weather meant that all the drivers and many spectators were covered in dust.

So, with increased traffic, road improvements had to be made. Thatcham High Street, then part of the

The Bath Road through Thatcham had been turnpiked around 1720 and at the western end of the village there was a toll-house, with a gate across the road until 1878. The toll-house (right) and adjoining cottage stood here until demolished in the 1960s.

The view looking east along the Bath Road at Thatcham 'Newtown' in around 1914 – although road traffic was increasing at this date there is little evidence of it in the photograph!

An unusual scene in the Broadway c.1910: a traction engine tows a house through the village en route to 'French Gardens', then kept by Miss Hughes-Jones; it was to accommodate her lady gardeners. In the background (right) is Charles Grunter's builders' yard.

Chapel Street corner looking east around the time of the First World War. The premises in the foreground were those of the Ashman brothers, one of whom was involved in setting up TRTS.

Bath Road, was kerbed and asphalted by May 1901, and this work was extended as far as Turnfields in Chapel Street by September 1902. From 1908, tar spraying on all main roads gathered momentum and the surface of the Bath Road was eventually transformed from white to black.

In this way the dust problem was solved – but at a price. Berkshire's County Surveyor reported in 1909 that the Bath Road continued to absorb large quantities of materials. That year, the County Council had finished spraying the main road through Thatcham and its sub-surveyor, Mr F. Davies, canvassed the village for voluntary subscriptions to fund more local road works.

Before the First World War, Newbury Rural District Council contracted out its road repair work to local firms but this became an increasingly heavy burden – in 1910, it announced that its expenditure on road repairs had doubled in just three years. In spite of all the expenditure, road maintenance barely kept pace with the growth in traffic.

In 1911, no less a person than the Prime Minister – Herbert Asquith – was being driven through Thatcham on his way back to Downing Street for a crisis meeting of the cabinet. His chauffeur-driven car was involved in an accident with cyclist Nellie Green at the junction of Northfield Road, leaving the poor girl with a fractured jaw, broken nose, gashed face – and unconscious.

She was taken to hospital in the car and – with specialist help sent by the Prime Minister – made a full recovery. At the suggestion of Newbury Rural District Council, a warning road sign was placed at the Bath Road–Northfield Road junction and Mr Hockley (the owner of the corner house there) was persuaded to trim his hedge to improve visibility for all road users at that point.

Off the main roads, improvements were even slower. The Broadway was not metalled and tarred until the summer of 1911 and Station Road not until the spring of 1914. The latter had always been liable to flooding in winter and was further damaged by the carriage of road building materials from Thatcham railway station (including tons of stone from Cranmore) up to the main road.

However, all the work seemed worthwhile by the eve of the First World War. It was reported at that time that the 'renewing of the Bath Road, after months of labour, is completed at last'. As a result of all the money and effort put into the project, a 'good road is now available from Newbury to Reading,' although there was still concern about a 'dangerous corner' in Thatcham.

Postwar, there was a rapid growth in freight road transport companies, including the local firm of Thatcham Road Transport Services from 1921. That meant heavier vehicles now used the local roads, resulting in higher expenditure on road maintenance. For instance, the County Council purchased just

A car crash at the top of the Broadway in around 1920 – the S-bend here from Chapel Street into the High Street claimed many victims, such as this car, which crashed into C.G. Brown's shop.

20,000 gallons of road tar in 1914 but nearly 290,000 gallons in 1922.

After the War too, the same 'dangerous corner' (an S-bend at the junction of the High Street and the Broadway) continued to worry the villagers. At the annual parish assembly in 1921, there was a request that the County Council introduce a speed limit here and put up warning signs for drivers. In the future, through traffic would be diverted away from the High Street altogether!

Of course, local drivers were not averse to attempting a burst of speed in their motorcars. One of them, who earned himself something of a reputation for doing so in his day, was Mr Charles George Brown. He had originally set up in Thatcham as a silversmith and watchmaker in 1882 and then began selling and repairing bicycles – he rode the first 'bone-shaker' seen in the village.

In 1911, C.G. Brown established an engineering works and garage at premises adjacent to the King's Head Inn. He was one of the first people in the village to own a car, which he used to drive around the locality on his 'clock-winding' duties. As an engineer, he became involved in installing industrial manufacturing plant and his activities took him up to 120 miles from Thatcham.

By the standards of the 1920s, many locals recall him as a fast driver. He is remembered 'in the fast motor cars of the day, with his peaked cap worn in the reverse position and kept in place by his goggles, his nose well down over the wheel, being quite oblivious to angry pedestrians gesticulating at the side of the road'.

During the inter-war years, Thatcham's 'dangerous corner' remained a source of growing concern as traffic levels on the Bath Road increased. Cars were said to be speeding through the village's 30mph limit at up to 50mph, resulting in numerous accidents, so

Mr J.M. Henry of Colthrop Mill owned one of the first cars to be seen on the village streets. His open topped Argyle is seen here parked in Thatcham High Street and is the centre of attention.

The top of the Broadway looking west into the High Street before the First World War. C.G. Brown began trading in clocks, watches and jewellery but even at this time his premises (right) have also become a 'Motor Garage'.

The Bath Road at Thatcham Newtown looking west in the inter-war years. St John's Road leads off left (foreground) and Beverley House (right distance), is where Beverley Close is today.

An early local motorist was Mr Charles George Brown, seen here in about 1914 with daughter May in his 3h.p. Benz car – it had a rear engine, was chain driven and completely open to the elements.

The view east along Chapel Street towards Reading and London in the 1930s. White lines and other road markings have yet to appear but with so little traffic they are not needed at this date.

The London Road leading east out of Thatcham in the 1930s. The signpost for Bucklebury marks the junction with Harts Hill Road (left) and that with Stoney Lane is alongside the Plough Inn (right).

various plans were made to deal with the problem.

In 1923, although Berkshire County Council put warning signs along the Bath Road through Thatcham, it would not establish a speed limit in the village. Numerous accidents on the narrow bends at each end of the High Street and near Henwick Lane in ensuing years did persuade it to widen the High Street but not extend the (by then) 30mph speed limit along the Bath Road.

From the 1920s, improvement schemes were undertaken on the Bath Road, including both road widening and bypass building, initially at the road's eastern end. It was not until the 1930s that improvements to the road were made west of Reading, and in 1936 the Ministry of Transport made the Bath Road a trunk road from London to Bristol, giving it the official designation A4.

Locally, proposals to give Thatcham a bypass were first aired in the 1920s and in the middle of that decade Berkshire County Council put forward plans for a southern bypass around the village. However, the Parish Council preferred a northern bypass and in 1925 unanimously supported a plan for a new village bypass, which would cut across Park Lane near to St Mary's School.

However, Mr Cyril Shepherd – the owner of the poultry farm which then stood where the Whitelands estate is today – did not want a bypass across his property and wrote a protest letter to the council saying so! Parish councillors agreed to carry out an inspection and report back but before long they were expressing doubts as to whether the village really needed a bypass.

In 1929, at a special parish assembly called to consider the proposed Thatcham bypass, the chairman (Mr Arthur Brown) described the scheme as 'an unnecessary expense and a great danger to the two schools in the village'. As well as passing close to both schools, it would also necessitate the demolition of numerous existing buildings and the creation of four new crossroads.

In 1932, in view of accidents that had recently occurred at the bottleneck at the western end of the High Street, the Parish Council suggested to the County Surveyor that it was necessary to widen the road here. Initially he vetoed the council's request but two years later – in August, 1934 – work started when a shop which jutted out into the road at that point was demolished.

However, the days of speeding on the public highway were numbered, obliging drivers to do their fast driving on the race track instead. One local

Thatcham's garage proprietor-cum-racing driver Harry Lester at the wheel of one his MG specials, c.1915.

The view east along Thatcham High Street in the 1950s. Amongst the many shops and pubs in the street at this time was the 'Crown', a public house that closed down in 1954.

driver who did so was Mr Harry Lester who came to Thatcham from Knebworth (Herts). He lived at Beggar's Roost, Bury's Bank Road but set up his own garage business, H. Lester (Cars 1951) Ltd, at 10 Bath Road. It was really little more than pumps and a workshop, but his real interest lay in motor racing.

In the early postwar days he raced modified MG sports cars, building his own vehicles by modifying production cars. He built his first Lester-MG in 1949, developing a sports car that was lighter and better handling than the standard MG TC – an ideal car for an amateur driver like himself.

Although Harry Lester did drive competitively, in races, a team of drivers calling themselves the 'Monkey Stable' usually drove his cars. They were named indirectly after Lester, who was a short man with broad shoulders and long arms – some people thought he was rather simian in appearance', it is said. Fortunately, Harry never discovered the origin of the team name!

The most successful season enjoyed by Lester-MG cars was in 1952, culminating in his cars winning all first three places in the 1500cc class of the first Goodwood Nine-Hours race in August. It was a season of exceptional success that the 'Monkey Stable' was never able to repeat. (Harry Lester continued to run his garage until he retired – he died at the age of 82 in 1982.)

After the Second World War, in 1951, the Deputy County Surveyor explained his plan for a short relief road around the north of Thatcham High Street to a Parish Council meeting. Numerous accidents proved the need for such a road, like the one in 1954, when a

Guinness tanker crashed into the front of the White Hart and flooded the hotel cellar with 1,000 gallons of stout!

The problem was solved when the relief road was built to the north of the High Street by Tilbury Construction, at a total cost of £54,000. Work began in November 1961, and by the spring of 1962 demolition work was under way along the line of the new road. One building to go was Messrs B.J. Brooks' corn store – built in 1925 – just off High Street in Park Lane (as it then was).

To allow pedestrians to cross the relief road, a subway was constructed. Its design was intended 'to reduce as much as possible the tunnel-like effect which to a certain extent is inevitable'. This was done by letting in as much daylight as possible and using light coloured panels designed by the County Surveyor and his staff. It was illuminated night and day by six electric lamps.

Work on the new road was completed nine days early and the Assistant County Surveyor (Mr G. Griffiths) congratulated the contractors for keeping 'right up to or in advance of their programme throughout'. No sooner had the relief road been opened to traffic, on Saturday 1 September 1962, than Newbury District Council closed Thatcham High Street to undertake sewage works!

As a reminder of just how busy local roads had become by this date, there was a nasty accident on the relief road the following Monday (3 September). A pedestrian, Mr Hubert Breach of Park Lane, was crossing the road when he was in collision with a van towing a horse box and suffered injuries which included a fractured skull. Even on the relief road

The western end of Thatcham's new relief road (looking east) shortly after it opened in 1962.

Thatcham High Street looking west in 1963 – after the new relief road had taken away the through traffic.

accidents still happened!

At this time there was still two-way traffic in Thatcham High Street and this was also a problem. Within weeks of the new road opening, complaints were being made about the 'dangerous turning' from the relief road into the western end of the High Street. The County Council felt that installing streetlights here would solve the problem although the Parish Council was not convinced.

In 1965 the County Surveyor proposed putting 'No Entry' signs at the western end of High Street and this plan was soon effected – a little inconvenient but much safer for drivers. At this date, the A4 through Thatcham still carried a heavy flow of London to Bristol traffic but since the mid-1950s there had been plans for a motorway from London to Bristol that would deal with this.

By 1967 work was underway at each end of the motorway but the middle section – through the scenic downlands of Berkshire and Wiltshire – proved highly controversial and was the subject of public enquiries. After much debate, its alignment was fixed and construction commenced. It opened as the M4 on 22 December 1971 and it took most long distance traffic away from Thatcham.

Local Bus and Coach Operators

The old village of Thatcham itself only really had one coach company, although there were others operating in the locality. One of the first was based 'up the hill' at Cold Ash. George Howlett lived at Cold Ash but kept the Oak Tree Garage, Bucklebury. In 1908 he set up a carrier-cum-bus service from Cold Ash to Newbury, using horse-drawn vehicles until 1914 when he purchased his first motor vehicle. About 1917 he also started a service to Reading and also undertook private hire work.

Albert Austin of Cold Ash became a bus proprietor in 1919 upon 'demob' from the army and purchased the Cold Ash–Newbury carrier-cum-bus service from George Howlett. However, the two men fell out when the latter again began operating on this route from October, 1922, in direct competition with one another, until Howlett was forced to give up this route in 1930.

William Pocock took over the post office stores on Cold Ash hill about 1903 and added a taxi business about 1920. When his sons joined him, the Cold Ash Garage was built adjacent to the shop. Their passenger carrying work expanded and by 1926 the Pococks were operating a small bus that was driven by Sid Coxhead, covering the service from Cold Ash to Newbury.

Albert Austin's bus at Newbury Wharf in the 1920s.

William Pocock's premises (left) on Cold Ash Hill.

123

Thatcham had half-a-dozen general carriers before the First World War. One of them was Fred Maslin. He started a two-horse daily passenger service to Newbury but introduced a Darracq motor vehicle on the route in April 1914. After war broke out, Fred Maslin enlisted in 1915, his business being taken over by 'Freddie' Spanswick, who came to Thatcham in that same year.

Frederick Spanswick was born at Aldbourne, Wiltshire, in 1877. As a young man, he went to live at Chaddleworth and traded there as a motor and cycle engineer before taking up residence at premises in Thatcham Broadway. Here, he is credited with developing Maslin's trade into a full motor coach establishment and reputedly running the first motor bus in the district.

At first, Spanswick ran a horse bus on the Thatcham–Newbury route but he introduced a Ford Model T van, with seating for 14 passengers, in 1919. With a canvas top and a reversible wooden Thatcham–Newbury destination board on the front, this vehicle was registered BL884. In his day, George (the Wanderer) Powell says the Thatcham–Newbury return fare was 6d.

Some locals recalled this vehicle, describing it as 'a lorry converted into a bus where the back axle was'. Spanswick '... put a sprocket on and made the chassis longer and put the back wheels there'. The back wheels were indeed chain-driven! It was painted grey with the words 'The Spanswick' on its sides and made two or three return trips into Newbury every day (excluding Sundays).

In the years after the First World War, bus and coach travel grew rapidly, both for regular services and annual outings. Many elderly inhabitants remember some of the early vehicles to be seen in and around Thatcham. One gentleman, George Powell – known as the Wanderer because he had travelled so much of West Berkshire – recalled many of the bus and coach firms to be seen on local roads during the inter-war years. He remembered vehicles with solid tyres and open seats upstairs.

Immediately after the war, buses and coaches belonging to numerous family businesses became a common sight on local roads. 'In no time at all along came Durnford's and Norton's', Powell recalled. 'Norton's had the hard tyres and open tops', he said, 'but Durnford's only ran to the seaside'. Indeed, the proprietor – Mr J.C. Durnford – who used to 'work for the doctor at Midgham Green', was one of the Newbury area's first coach proprietors; 'he bought a charabanc and moved to Newbury and that was how he started', we are told.

A charabanc outing from Thatcham in the late 1920s. Passengers include Mr and Mrs Harry Goodman (far left) and Mr and Mrs Broughton (centre).

Villagers on charabanc outing in the early 1920s. Passengers include Gertrude Collins (back row, in hat and dark glasses); Fred Farley (second left, with moustache and hat); George Ralph (in sailor uniform); Olive Lyford (second right back row, in light hat); and Mr and Mrs Charles Lyford (centre front, both in hats).

Members of St Mary's Church choir on another charabanc outing from Thatcham in about 1930. Left to right, they include Mr and Mrs Fyfield, Eva Fyfield, Miss Cousens, Joan Staccini, Ron Hale (hatless), Wilf Phillips and Mr Legge.

A coach outing from Thatcham at Southsea in the early 1930s. The shed behind their coach is signed 'City of Portsmouth Car Park'.

Charles Durnford had served an apprenticeship as a motor mechanic and started a transport business from his base near Woolhampton in 1920. He was joined in the venture by his four sons and the firm undertook all sorts of haulage work, not just coach excursions, although it is true that from the 1923 season Charles Durnford & Sons' slogan was that their coaches 'go to the seaside every day'! Southsea was the easiest seaside town for these early vehicles to reach in a day, there and back.

Freddie Spanswick sometimes found himself in competition with other operators on the route. In 1923 he came up against 'Norton's Motor Service', which operated early double-decker buses and was popular with local passengers. Spanswick was obliged to purchase two purpose-built buses of his own (a Ford and a Morris), painting them in a more attractive blue and white livery.

Spanswick's buses were smaller but faster than Norton's which won him back the patronage of Thatcham folk, increasing his share of traffic to the extent that he had to recruit more drivers. One of them, George Amor, soon found out how serious the competition could be whilst engaged in a little 'leapfrogging', when a heavier Norton bus was deliberately rolled back into his own!

Nevertheless, Spanswick's buses eventually saw off all the competition on the route (Norton's withdrew in 1928). By this time, Spanswick had added to his fleet and developed an extensive private hire and excursion trade along with the service work. In 1930, he held licences for tours to over a dozen destinations including Oxford, Swindon, Salisbury, Windsor and Weymouth.

Many enjoyable excursions were taken by villagers in charabancs and coaches in the 1920s and 1930s. These included outings organised by the local Methodist Church 'mums and toddlers' group of the time, which called itself the 'Women's Bright Hour'. The group was founded about 1930 by and for the ladies of the church following a visit to the church by an evangelist named the Revd Brackenbury.

Two notable founder members were Mrs Edith Collins and Mrs Matilda Bosley. The group eventually had about 40 members and held regular Tuesday afternoon meetings at the Methodist Church in Chapel Street. 'Membership cost 1d. a week', remembered Mrs Evelyn Hutchins, 'and the ladies put their coins onto the penny-plate, which was brought round at their meetings'. Subscriptions included the cost of a cup of tea and a biscuit, but for their annual trip to the seaside the ladies paid in a few pence a week during the year. St Mary's Church choir also had an annual outing.

By 1930 there were various coach operators in the Newbury area who ran both local services and seaside excursions. For example, on Saturday 27 June 1936, a fleet of Newbury & District coaches took the engineering staff at Thatcham Board Mills and 121 workers from the British Floorcloth Company to Bognor Regis for their annual outing. However, the favourite seaside resort for local folk was always Southsea.

With the passing of the Road Traffic Act of 1930, the smaller coach operators realised that co-operation, not competition, was to their advantage. Accordingly, most West Berkshire operators amalgamated into The Newbury & District Motor Services Ltd (N&D) from 1932. Under an agreement dated 23 January 1933, N&D acquired Spanswick's business for £1,800 in cash and shares.

Freddie Spanswick joined N&D, becoming their Rolling Stock Superintendent. He resigned when the N&D was sold to the Red and White Coach Company in January 1944. In retirement he was remembered as a staunch churchman, very fond of music and a member of St Mary's Church choir. He died at his home in Thatcham Broadway on 25 May 1952, aged 75 years.

Thatcham Road Transport Services

The later history of Colthrop Mill would not be complete without some mention of the transport company that became part of the complex during the inter-war years. Many will remember it as the Cropper & Colthrop Transport Company or perhaps as Reed Transport when in ownership of the Reed Paper Group, but the transport business at Colthrop all began in a modest way here in the village of Thatcham after the First World War.

A village family, the Ashmans, were leather-workers here in the late-nineteenth century. Two sons of George and Fanny Ashman – Frank and Sydney – had business premises adjacent to the King's Head making shoes and horsewear respectively. As the demand for saddlery and harnesses declined in the early-twentieth century – with the growth in motor transport – the latter brother seems to have decided that if you can't beat 'em, join 'em!

Sydney Ashman entered the road transport business in the village in 1919. He purchased a single vehicle – a Saurer lorry – and undertook haulage work for Colthrop Mill. However, financial rewards for such work were poor and he soon switched to general haulage instead and entered into a business partnership.

His partner was Wilfred Street, who had been born at Burnley in Lancashire but found his way to Thatcham after serving as a sergeant instructor (engineering) with the Royal Flying Corps in the war. The pair had first met in 1920 and in June of the following year went into partnership, setting up the firm of Thatcham Road Transport Services (TRTS).

The business was based in a garage at the top of Thatcham Broadway opposite Sydney Ashman's erstwhile saddlery. The pair now ran a Sentinel

Sydney Ashman, co-founder of TRTS is seen here (right), outside the saddlery and harness-making premises, which he kept with his brother Frank prior to establishing the haulage firm.

Sydney Ashman's and Wilf Street's original TRTS premises at the top of Thatcham Broadway, c.1921.

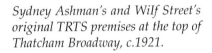

After TRTS moved to Colthrop, this filling station was opened on the A4 at Colthrop Lane.

TRTS became part of BRS in the postwar years, and one of its vehicles is seen in the pulp shed at Colthrop c.1950 with some employees. Left to right: Nat Aldridge, Charlie Smith, Micky Hunt, Pat Oswald, Terry Hartnett and Ken Moore.

Wilfred Street, co-founder of TRTS became Lieutenant Colonel of T Company South Midland Home Guard Transport Column, based in Oxford but with a depot at Colthrop. There were about 200 in the Home Guard's TRTS division, some of whom are seen here during the Second World War.

steam lorry and gradually built up a fleet of similar vehicles – they had 27 of them before the decade was out. However, the internal combustion engine soon replaced steam both nationally and locally.

TRTS began switching to petrol and diesel lorries from 1930 and moved to new premises around the same time. Back in 1924 the firm had acquired a further site in Colthrop Lane, using both until 1935, when all vehicles operated from here. TRTS had built itself a brand new brick and concrete depot at Colthrop for all its lorries by 1937.

Upon the outbreak of the Second World War, TRTS found itself responsible not just for its own fleet but also for 62 Bedford trucks stationed at local Army camps, and (like transport firms generally) came under the overall control of the Ministry of War Transport. TRTS had to provide drivers and undertake vehicle maintenance work.

Colthrop became home to the South Midland Home Guard Transport Column, made up of local men plus drivers from Abingdon, Reading and as far afield as Oxford, providing essential transport for men and materials throughout the war years. To provide refreshments for these drivers between duties, the Thatcham Home Guard Club was born.

Newbury magistrates were approached for a special club licence so that drivers could be served with alcoholic drinks! The Column was based at the TRTS Colthrop depot, and Wilf Street became its Lieutenant-Colonel, commanding the Home Guard for a wide area round about. There were 200 men in just the TRTS Home Guard division alone.

Under the postwar Labour government, road transport was nationalised and TRTS became part of British Road Services – Colthrop was a sub-depot of BRS's Reading depot. The vehicle fleet was repainted from dark blue to red. A change of government saw denationalisation, and Colthrop's 89 lorries were bought for £225,000 in October 1954.

The new owner was the 'Cropper & Colthrop Transport Co.' which many people will remember. As directors, Sydney Ashman and Wilfred Street were back at the helm, but not for long, because the Reed Group took over the Colthrop complex from 1956. Colthrop's lorries were repainted green as part of the Reed Transport fleet, by October 1960.

By this time, Sydney Ashman had retired – he died at Padworth in 1964 aged 80. Having retired in 1956, Wilfred Street lived at Henwick and died in 1985 at the age of 87. Interestingly, it was in that same year that the original TRTS building at Colthrop was demolished but the building once used by TRTS at the top of the Broadway still stands.

Colthrop's vehicle fleet was housed in a new depot at the bottom of Colthrop Lane from 1984 and further changes of ownership occurred. After Swedish company SCA purchased the Board Mill in 1991 the lorries were repainted dark blue – the livery that had been used in 1921. Sydney Ashman and Wilf Street would have been pleased!

Chapter X1

The Sporting Life

A History of Thatcham Cricket Club

The history of the game in Old Thatcham goes back over two centuries in its origins. Early reports relating to cricket in Thatcham, for example, show that cricket was then played on The Marsh (Dunstan Green). On Wednesday 19 July 1786, a cricket match took place between two unnamed gentlemen, 'for a considerable sum'. One man got 135 notches (runs) and the other 125. It was estimated that in the course of three hours' play, the loser ran 25 miles and the winner 20 miles. The mileage was reduced with team games of course!

Records show that team matches were taking place on Thatcham's Marsh in the eighteenth century. Early matches may have been annual events – for instance, on 9 July 1789, 'a grand match of cricket' was played here between Thatcham and Newbury. Then, in the following year, on Friday 9 July 1790, again 'for a considerable sum', another match was played 'between the gentlemen of Newbury and those of Thatcham'. There may have been other unreported matches here too.

On Sunday 28 July 1793, a cricket match was played at The Marsh between 'a party of Thatcham, and a party of Newbury'. In the end, Thatcham won by four wickets, although they then had to take on the same team away, at the Newbury Marsh (Northcroft), in a return fixture scheduled for Monday 18 August 1793.

By the mid-nineteenth century, during the reign of Queen Victoria, a cricket team was playing regularly throughout the season on Thatcham Marsh. It was named the Thatcham Victoria Cricket Club and was certainly functioning by 1860. The earliest extant score sheet is for a home match on Thursday 27 June

1867, relating to a game between Thatcham and Wickham cricket teams. A two innings game – typical for the time – the result was a seven wicket win for the home side!

During the year 1881, the name of Thatcham's then cricket club was changed and it became simply the Thatcham Cricket Club. The season was a mixed one: at the start, there was a game between Thatcham Victoria and Lamborne (away), which the opposition won easily, although there was an 'enjoyable evening afterwards'. In mid-season, when Kingsclere played our village team on The Marsh, it was called Thatcham (late Victoria) and on this occasion beat the visiting side.

Thatcham took on old rivals Wickham at an away match later in 1881 and this time it proved an easy victory for the opposition. This may have been a sign that all was not well with the club for in the next few years cricket in Thatcham went into decline and was described as being in 'somewhat of a languishing condition'. By 1886, however, 'fresh interest was infused' and the team won their first match of that season, the executive (Committee) taking this as a promising omen.

At a meeting at the New Inn in Chapel Street, they determined to improve things. Practices were set up for Mondays, Wednesdays and Saturdays. A new committee was appointed, with Thatcham's vicar, Revd Hezekiah Martin, as President and Mr A.S. Denness as Captain; other members John Wallen (Secretary), Tom Diggens (Collector), Fred Hyde (Treasurer), with Henry Smith, William Fairthorne, Charles Randall, Ambrose White and Edward Mathews (Committee).

Within a few years, the Thatcham Cricket Club was on the way up again. At the start of the 1892 season a special meeting of the club was held at the White Hart at which it was resolved to enter the team for the Compton Cup. This was a challenge cup offered by Compton CC in order to encourage cricket in Berkshire parishes. Only parish residents were allowed in village teams and the Thatcham team was chosen in a selection game between players under and over 30 years.

Thatcham played Compton on the Downs at what was the first match for the cup in the 1892 season. Thatcham won the toss and – in 'boisterous' weather – elected to bat first. In their innings, Thatcham notched up 102 runs: top scorer was their captain, A.S. Denness, with 23, followed by three of his team-mates (G. House, H. Fullbrook and the Hon. Tollemache) who each scored 18. The then vicar of

Home ground to Thatcham Cricket Club – and others! The Marsh (Dunstan Green), with gypsies camped on it around 1900.

129

Thatcham, Revd David Pierce, was a 'playing president' but did not get any runs.

Compton's innings was 'a very poor performance' and in reply they only managed 78 runs, their top scorer being J. Haigh with 26. Thatcham were the eventual victors by an innings and four runs. It was described as a very enjoyable game, with many spectators being present; lunch was supplied by Mr H. Pickard, of the Lamb Hotel, East Ilsley. Thatcham's winning streak continued – they went on to beat Bradfield on The Marsh the following week and then defeated other local village teams.

The composition of the Thatcham cricket team in the late nineteenth century remained rather a 'gentlemanly' affair. Apart from the Hon. Tollemache and the Revd Pierce, the other players were from proprietorial families. Charles Bolton kept the Swan Inn, John Shepherd was a wheelwright and Charles Wheeler was a blacksmith. Others were the sons of such – Edward Mathews' father kept Hatchgate Farm whilst Henry Fullbrook's was a barber and Henry Pinnock's a woodturner.

Thatcham Cricket Club spent the first half of the twentieth century searching for the perfect pitch. The team saw the facilities enjoyed by other cricket clubs when they played away – their opponents played on either well-manicured village greens or at pitches on country estates, which highlighted the shortcomings of their own pitch on The Marsh (Dunstan Green).

For away matches, it was necessary to borrow a donkey cart from a Mr Pratt. The club's gear and the players' kit were conveyed on this whilst team members travelled alongside on their bicycles. That drinking took place after matches is evidenced by the fact that in 1913 club members were fined by Newbury Magistrates for being drunk in charge of their donkey cart!

For home games, the pitch on The Marsh had to be prepared and on match days a marquee was hired, erected and returned after the game. The master of the nearby Bluecoat School, Mr Samuel Vallis – a keen cricketer – got his pupils to roll and cut the pitch beforehand. However, when war broke out in 1914 Mr Vallis and many other local men enlisted for the duration.

Things other than sport occupied the minds of Thatcham men for the next few years but after the First World War the thoughts of many of them turned again to cricket. In 1919, Thatcham Cricket Club was established in its present form and during the summer months matches were again played on The Marsh. However, the inadequacies of this pitch now became a real issue.

The Marsh was a long-established open space regarded as public property by the inhabitants of Thatcham – and others, such as the gypsies who often camped here. It was a children's playground, a site for all sorts of games and for the annual village bonfire on 5 November. Other public events took place here, including such things as the holding of circuses from time to time.

The rough condition of the ground was not conducive to good cricket – the long-grassed outfield in particular restricted high scoring. Thus in 1920, the then-secretary of Thatcham Cricket Club, Mr H.H. Brooks, wrote to the Parish Council asking for permission to enclose a part of The Marsh – measuring 25 yards long and either 10 yards or 5 yards wide – as a cricket pitch.

Thatcham Parish Council agreed to the club enclosing a 25x5 yard area for cricket, but it was a short-lived pitch. In 1921 the club moved to a new ground on the east side of Park Lane although this was far from ideal. They were kept off this pitch for a time when the field had to be ploughed up for haymaking, and other events made some seasons particularly memorable.

In 1923, for instance, Thatcham faced Kingsclere, always a side they found hard to beat. To the delight of the home crowd, Thatcham got the benefit of a dubious umpiring decision to which the home spectators responded so enthusiastically they inflamed matters. The visiting players began to leave the pitch and the Thatcham captain had to persuade them to finish the game.

In August, 1923, Thatcham took on local rivals Newbury and soundly defeated them, winning by seven wickets. The 'man of the match' was Jack Campbell, an exceptionally fast bowler, who took seven Newbury wickets in the second innings. Other Thatcham players included Messrs Cyril Barr, Fred Davies, Geoff Witts, Frank Ashman, and brothers Vincent and Bobby Brown.

In 1925, the club moved to a better ground on the western side of Park Lane. Here, the team played some superb cricket in the early 1930s. In 1930, for example, Cyril Barr scored a record 175 runs in a single innings. During the 1931 season Thatcham set two more records with scores of 257 against High Wycombe and – just weeks later – 266 against Whitchurch (Oxfordshire).

In the 1930s too, Thatcham Cricket Club added new players to their team, such as Max Langdon, Howard Peters, Jim Vallis and Captain Tom Webb MBE – he lived in Station Road and was club secretary by 1935. Sadly, the good times came to an end in 1939 when the club's activities were suspended and its pitch ploughed up in the wartime 'dig for victory' campaign.

After the war, Thatcham's recreational needs were a priority and a playing-field project was set up under a voluntary group named the Memorial Playing Fields Association. Funds were raised by public subscription: the president of Thatcham Cricket Club, Mr A.S.B. Tull of Crookham House. donated £500 and the club received £125 in compensation for the loss of its old pitch.

Thatcham Cricket Club c.1920. The umpire (back row, right) is Reg Durbidge. Players include George Davies, Les Mason, George Harris, Harry Pearson, Oliver Rich and Bill Oram (boy on right).

Thatcham Cricket Club c.1930. Left to right, back row: *? Haines (umpire), Sidney Ashman, Stanley Brown, Capt. Webb, Bill Clippendale, Ray Onion, Howard Peters, Tommy Fisher (scorer);* front row: *Max Langdon, Cyril Barr, Jim Vallis, Bobby Brown, Fred Davis.*

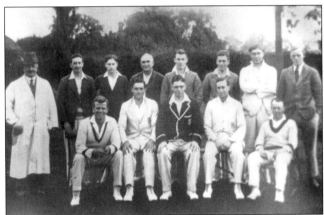

Thatcham Cricket Club's 2nd XI for the 1948 season. Left to right, back row: *John Holbon, Cyril Bartholomew, Eric Eastman, Peter House, Jack Brooks, Richard Watts, John Wimbush, 'Tankie' Smith;* front row: *Owen Digweed, Ross Arnold, Max Langdon, Charlie Smith, Jack Wheeler, Bernard Spanswick.*

Thatcham Cricket Club, c.1960. Left to right, back row: *John Holbon (umpire), Harry Barrett, Johnny Mann, Barry Dolton, Harry Tweedy, John Wimbush, Gordon Barr, Norman Peel;* front row: *Sidney Norwood, Peter Holloway, Jack Brooks, Percy Davies, Clifford Fry;* boy at front: *Keith Davies.*

Land north of the Bath Road was purchased from the Brown family and a new Memorial Playing Field was opened here in 1947. There was a condition attached that it should be used only for organised games, one of which was cricket. Club members worked to create what became one of the finest cricket pitches in the south of England. It looked like their search was over.

After the Second World War, Thatcham Cricket Club found itself a new home at the Memorial Playing Fields where it at last had a pitch that was second to none. Here, the club played its home games in matches against other local village teams but also entertained more prestigious teams in county matches and benefit games, of which there were several during the 1950s.

One of the most memorable benefit games took place in coronation year (1953), when the fifteenth of a series to mark the achievements of Alec Bedser (whose bowling in the five Test matches that year helped England regain the Ashes) was held in Thatcham. A crowd of 5,000 people turned up from all over the country to see their England heroes play in the benefit match.

Bedser's XI included some of his England and Surrey team-mates, such as Peter May, Tony Lock and Jim Laker. Former Surrey captain H.M. Garland Wells led the opposing team, which had Ben Barnett of Australia, F.M. Worrell of the West Indies, Robin Marlar (Sussex) and John Warr (Middlesex) in its ranks, along with E. Underdown, film actor and well-known amateur jockey.

Thatcham's players were excellent hosts, making their new pitch available for the special match – it was deemed little short of county standard. The hosts also planned the seating, catering and other arrangements. There was a holiday atmosphere at the game and the cricket was not taken too seriously – the crowd had really come to see the celebrities present in the village that day.

In the course of six hours' play, over 600 runs were scored. Sixes were hit to all corners of the ground, among the crowd, over the pavilion and one hit a car parked near the refreshment marquee. Garland Wells's XI batted first and amassed a total of 317 for 7 before declaring. In reply, Alec Bedser's XI were still ten runs short of this total when the stumps were drawn to end the game.

The event raised around £600 for the Bedser benefit fund. Various items were auctioned, such as the bats used in test matches and the autographs of famous sporting personalities – one such was that of champion jockey Sir Gordon Richards. Alec Bedser himself had only to poke his head out of the pavilion and he was hounded by hordes of young cricket fans clamouring for his autograph.

Local cricket was marked by ups and downs as it continued on its seasonal basis, with derby matches against Newbury being especially competitive. In 1962, Thatcham lost to their local rivals at Northcroft for the first time in 16 years. However, at home in 1969, Thatcham got 205 for 0 in reply to Newbury's 247 for 1 in a match when only one wicket fell and 3 players scored centuries.

Thatcham's Memorial Playing Field continued to be run entirely by voluntary efforts until 1972 when financial difficulties resulted in the Parish Council assuming control but problems of an unexpected nature arose. The Whitelands estate was then being built and residents began using the playing-fields for access – walking and riding bicycles across the cricket pitch in the process!

During a match against Hungerford in July of that year, a family out for an afternoon stroll – complete with a baby in a pushchair – brought the game to a halt. Asked to move on, the father refused, claiming that as a Thatcham ratepayer he had every right to be there. When play resumed, the amazed visitors were all out for 136. In reply, Thatcham won the game by three wickets.

The 1970s was a time of mixed fortunes for Thatcham Cricket Club. The team had some excellent players in the likes of Harry Barrett, John Wimbush and Pete Holloway. In 1973, the club entered league cricket, joining Division 2 of the Hampshire League. However, the ground problems continued – within a few years the pitch was a mess and the pavilion was vandalised.

Players resigned and the club was relegated in 1974 and 1975. There was talk of disbanding, but it was decided to carry on, with new players such as Frank Bird, Derek Eggbeer and Andrew Mills. In 1976, captain Cliff Fry and John Hawley both scored centuries so the club was promoted. Then the club was warned that it might be banned from the league because of its poor pitch in 1977.

Following an approach from the club that year, Thatcham Town Council provided funds to improve the pitch as long as club members supplied the labour. In 1979 a longer-term solution was effected

The clocktower erected at the Memorial Playing Fields, which were opened in 1947 for 'organised' games only.

when the council purchased from the Brown family a meadow (Brownsfield) adjacent to the Memorial Playing Field. A new pitch was laid out and a new pavilion built here in 1980.

Thatcham Cricket Club played its last season on the Memorial Playing Field in 1981 and moved to Brownsfield thereafter. The 1982 season saw Derek Eggbeer set a new club and league record by taking 10 wickets for 39 runs and John Gourlay resurrected the colts to train up future players.

In 1986, the club joined the Berkshire League and in 1988 won the Bowness West Berkshire Knock-out Trophy. Thatcham had another excellent season in 1989, completing a double by retaining the Bowness Trophy. They won their division and were unbeaten with Frank Bird and Vic Pye setting a division record partnership of 152 runs unbeaten.

Success continued into the 1990s, and in five seasons of Berkshire League cricket the club won 6 championships and set 8 league records. Thatcham Town Cricket Club now plays regularly at Brownsfield and by the year 2000 the club had four senior sides and a number of colts sides; its teams play in the Thames Valley League, the Berkshire League and the Borders Sunday League.

The Rise of Thatcham Football Club

Thatcham has a long sporting tradition, going way back into Victorian times when teams of local lads kicked a ball around on The Marsh (Dunstan Green). However, organised football was only established about a century ago – Thatcham Football Club played its first recorded match in 1894.

At that time, the club played its games on The Marsh and used the Plough Inn as its base, holding an annual dinner there at the end of each season. Thatcham was then captained by Harry Wells, who played left back; J. Palmer was right back and the goalkeeper was D. Bushell. Others who played in the early years included Messrs Allen, Dennis, Maccabee and Hunt (half backs); Bosley and Brooks (right wing forwards); Carter and Heaver (left wing forwards); and O'Riley (centre forward).

There are old photographs in existence of TFC teams in days gone by. The oldest I have in my collection is for the 1895/6 season and shows the team (made up from the individuals named above) at the end of that season. It was judged to have been 'very satisfactory', with 105 goals for and 31 against in 24 matches. The best games that season had been

The TFC team of 1895/6 (probably at the Plough Inn) – the players included captain Harry Wells and D. Bushell (goalkeeper). This was only the second season of the club's existence.

The Thatcham Lads Football Club team, 1913/14. The goalkeeper was Leonard Durbidge.

The TFC team of 1935/6, with their cups – front row: Cyril Barr (captain) and Les Attfield (goalkeeper).

The TFC team of 1919/20. Back row, second from right: Richard White. Front row, second from right: Albert Nightingale.

Players and officials involved in the annual Vic French Memorial Match, c.1960. The match saw 'old players' take on the current team players. Included in the picture are: 'Digger' Blisset, Billy Wilkins, Jock Hutchinson, Norman Hall, Jack Brooks, Percy Davies, Jim Thirkill, Jack Davies, John Lloyd, Bob Smith, Eric Fisher, David Molloy, Cyril Bartholomew, Sam Aldridge, George Slade, Gordon Bowden, Birt Claridge, John Holbon (referee).

against Reading Strollers, Maidenhead Temperance, Newbury Reserves and – although Thatcham lost the match – Wantage (in the Berks and Bucks Junior Cup Competition).

From the First World War period onwards, key players at that time included Richard White and Albert Nightingale and goalkeeper Leonard Durbidge. By the 1930s, the TFC captain was Cyril Barr and the goalkeeper was Les Attfield.

A mainstay of sport – especially football – in Thatcham during the early years was Frederick (Freddy) Davis, born in 1884. He worked for 15 years for TRTS but was a carpenter by trade and often assisted backstage at village concerts and shows. He was also a special police constable.

In his younger days he gave some dazzling performances on the football field for TFC. Of only slight build, his agility was such that his tricks and wiles often nonplussed burly full backs on the opposing team. In later life he became a referee and earned a reputation as a no-nonsense official with the Berks and Bucks League.

Freddy Davis was an able football administrator locally and helped to set up the Thatcham Minors Football Team in 1937. As well as playing football for

Thatcham, he also played for Thatcham Cricket Club. Sadly, he died in June 1948, aged 64 years, but his sons Jack and Percy became local footballers of note.

Thatcham Football Club won the Senior Cup in the Reading Challenge Cup Competition in the 1935/6, 1947/8, 1949/50 and 1950/1 seasons. The 1935/6 season was particularly good for the club, which played 42 games altogether, 26 of them in the Reading and District Premier League.

Of the latter, TFC won all but three of their games and picked up no less than four cups that season. These were the Berks and Bucks Junior Cup, the Reading Town Senior Cup, the Newbury Challenge (Graystone) Cup and the Ben Warner Cup (for a one-off game between Thatcham and Newbury football clubs).

With the success of TFC after the Second World War came the search for a new ground. The club purchased land off Northfield Road in 1948 and first played on this new pitch in 1952. Known as Lancaster Close, the new pitch was used for hundreds of TFC matches over the next 40 years.

The Lancaster Close ground was eventually sold to West Berkshire Housing Association for £982,500 and given over to housing development. The income was

Thatcham Minors team, 1963/4. Players include – back row: Eddie Denness (trainer), Malcolm Broughton, Leon Sheldon, Colin Fox, Dennis Keylock, Joe Freeman, Dennis Keogh; front row: Colin Young, Bernard Keylock, Vic Pye, Tony Ayres, Mick Dunbar, Chris Doyle.

used to finance the building of a modern football ground south of Thatcham, at Waterside Park. This was constructed by Northfield Developments at a cost of £952,500 and was first used for a match on Boxing Day, 26 December 1992. In the 1990s Thatcham Town FC played in the Wessex League – winning the League Championship in 1996 and the League Cup on a record four occasions.

Some Members of a Sporting Family

The Hunts are an old Thatcham family who can trace their ancestry back to John Hunt, of Ham in Wiltshire, who set up a charity in Thatcham over 400 years ago. More recent generations of the family have left their mark on the place through their sporting achievements, notably in athletics and football during the first half of the twentieth century.

The contribution of one branch of the family was recounted for me by the late Bert Hunt. His father (Herbert 'Micky' Hunt) was born in Kingsclere but, when only a few months old, moved with his family to Thatcham late in the nineteenth century. They lived at 39 The Broadway, one of the Hunt charity cottages, where Micky lived out most of the rest of his life. He attended the Bluecoat School and served in Salonika with the RASC during the First World War, being mentioned in dispatches for bravery.

Searching for work after the war, Micky moved to Wales for a time and became a miner. He was a keen footballer and played professionally for Ton Pentre in the 1920/1 season. It was in Wales that he met and married his wife Mary, before returning to Thatcham. He worked on a farm for a while and then at Reeds, where he was a crane driver for 39 years.

During the 1920s Micky Hunt became coach to the athlete Frank Close, who was only 15 when this training began. He was coached on Thatcham Moors – 'at Frank Adams' running meadow' – and also on long distance stints around Crookham and Greenham Commons. Bert Hunt recalled going with a busload of supporters when Frank Close won a ten-mile cross-country championship away at Beaconsfield in about 1930 – as shown in the accompanying photograph.

In the 1930s, Frank went on to become one of Britain's finest athletes. The peak of his career as a runner was when he competed in the 1936 Olympic Games in Berlin – to which Micky Hunt went along as his trainer and coach. Micky was himself a good athlete and footballer, playing for Thatcham for many years. He retired from Reeds in 1961 but played football in a veterans' match when he was 70! After a short illness, he died aged 79 in September 1974.

The contribution of another branch of the family was recalled for me by Cecil Hunt. His father – Charles 'Harry' Hunt, brother of Micky – was also born in Kingsclere but came to Thatcham and made 5 Hollington Place (off Green Lane) his family's home. He worked at Colthrop Mill and was twice married (his first wife died in childbirth); his second wife, Louisa, was mother to Cecil.

Harry Hunt was another keen athlete who – in his day – played both football and cricket, earning a reputation as a spin bowler for Thatcham Cricket Club. Sadly, he died aged 62 in March 1939. His own family of nine boys (and two girls) included several

The runner Frank Close (centre) is feted as cross country champion at Beaconsfield, c.1930. His trainer was Mr Herbert 'Micky' Hunt (left).

The TFC Minors team, 1947/8. Left to right, back row: *Harry Hunt, Don Tyler, Bob Arnold, Graham Tillen, John Blundy, Hugh Martin, Tom Tidbury (secretary);* front row: *Peter Smith, Peter Digweed, Keith Armstrong, Dennis Bishop, Cecil Hunt, Les Goddard, Denis Haines.*

Left: *St Mary's School senior relay teams at a Home Guard fête in 1946.* Left to right, back row: *Les Goddard, ? Styles, ? Newland, Keith Armstrong;* front row: *John Preston, Daphne Taylor, Mr Shaw (headmaster), Cecil Hunt, ? Tuthill.*

Below: *A sack football match under way in a field at Thatcham Farm (looking north to Green Lane), c.1947. Players, left to right: Ron Townsend, Cecil Hunt (back to camera), David Molloy, Russell Hunt (on ground), John Tyler, Arthur Collins, Les Goddard.*

sons who became well-known local footballers and who were trained as such by their father on Thatcham Moors. Among them were Tom, Leonard (Podge), William (Bill) and Russell – the latter went on to play in goal for Thatcham's first team.

Cecil attended St Mary's School in Park Lane along with a number of other lads whose passion was football and who played in the Thatcham minors' team after the Second World War. The minors' team was the future of the village's first team which three of its players duly went on to represent in later years, Cecil amongst them.

In the immediate postwar years, the Thatcham minors' team played on what is now the Memorial Playing Field. Its goalkeeper was Graham Tillen, with Keith Armstrong at inside right – they used to practise their skills with a medicine ball if nothing else was available. Keith later played county football for Berks and Bucks whilst Graham became wicket keeper for Thatcham Cricket Club in the 1950s (and later club secretary). Although Cecil played in Thatcham Football Club's first team with Keith and Graham, he admitted he was never quite as good as them.

All three recalled their days with the minors, particularly the 1947/8 season, when the minors were runners-up in the Newbury and District Minors' Cup. The Thatcham team was beaten 6–2 in the final that year by Northcroft. Cecil recalled that for Thatcham's Football Club, like most others, the postwar years were an important time as it looked to the future: 'A generation had been lost to the war and we learnt a lot from the older players who trained us very well'.

On a lighter note, some of the younger players from the postwar years are shown in another photograph, playing 'sack football' at a village fête on a field (since built on) at Lower Way in about 1947.

Organisations and Festivities

Thatcham's Scouts and Guides

The Scout movement nationally began in the years before the First World War and in West Berkshire a meeting was held in October 1909, to form a committee for the co-ordination of Scouting in this area. One member of that committee was Major Charles Turner of Thatcham House, a local JP and Deputy Lieutenant of Berkshire – there were already some Scout troops operating in the county at that time but there is no record of one in Thatcham itself.

Scouting in the village of Thatcham is first mentioned in 1926. At that date, a 30th Newbury (Thatcham) Scout Group existed but so many boys were applying to become members that a ballot had to be held to select them – 24 of the applicants were chosen, plus eight others over the age of 18 years. A Mr Rogers was Scoutmaster and Mr A. Allen and Mr D. Boggitt were appointed assistant Scoutmasters.

Mr John Henry of Colthrop Mill agreed to advance the money for uniforms for the boys, which they could pay back in time; further, he made a donation of £5 and allowed the Scouts the use of the sports club hut. Mr Henry became president of the group, with Mr Arthur Brown as chairman and Mr Thomas Davies as treasurer. Unfortunately, there is no further record of the activities of the 30th Newbury (Thatcham) Scout Group.

However, in January 1935, an open Scout group was formed in the village and registered as the 43rd Newbury (Thatcham) Scout Group. The group's first Scoutmaster was the (then) headmaster of the Council School, Mr Reginald Lanning of The Laurels, Chapel Street. It had 25 members, who first met in an outbuilding in the garden of one of the boy's parents, although the Church of England Infant School later became its headquarters.

In 1938 a hut was erected on land off Church Gate, Lower Way (where the local Scout headquarters is today). This hut was used as an extra classroom for some of the many children evacuated to Thatcham during the Second World War. By 1941, the

Thatcham Girl Guides on their annual outing to Wittering, Sussex, in 1929. Their captain at this time was Miss 'Millicent' Buller-Turner of Thatcham House.

Scoutmaster of the group was Mr Eddie llsley of St George's Avenue, Newbury, and his assistant Scoutmaster was the Revd Dixon of Benham Hill. The Cubmaster was Mr E. Parsloe of Andover Road, Newbury and his assistant Scoutmaster was Mr N. Maccabee of Bartholomew Street, Newbury. As the Scout leaders went off into military service, however, the group began to decline.

It was revived after the war by Thatcham's vicar, Revd Bernard Thackeray, who became its Scoutmaster (continuing in this role until 1969). On 1 September 1945, the 43rd Newbury (Thatcham) group changed its name and became the 1st Thatcham Scout Group. It was now sponsored by St Mary's Church and thus restricted its entry to boys who were members of the Church of England. In 1947 the group was re-registered as the 1st Thatcham (St Mary's) Scout Group. Two years later, one of its members – Scout Richard Axford – stopped a runaway horse and was awarded the Gilt Cross for Gallantry by the Scout Association.

In the 1950s, the Scout hut was used by local schools as a classroom to accommodate 'overspill' pupils; Newbury Rural District Council criticised its 'insanitary arrangements' in August 1955, but it continued in use as such until the end of the decade. By the mid-1960s, membership of the 1st Thatcham Scout Group had dwindled to just one troop of half-a-dozen boys. However, in 1967 a new leader, Ray Frankland, took over. Then, in 1969, a local farmer offered the Scouts a replacement hut free of charge – but it was an ex-army hut at Bagshot, Surrey! With their new leader, Thatcham's Scouts set about dismantling it (and others, as part of the deal) before it was conveyed to the Church Gate site with the help of Reed Transport where it was re-erected at

a cost of £750.

The work took nearly four years to complete and just three weeks before the official opening the hut was destroyed by a 'mystery fire' one night in October 1972 – arson was suspected. Damage done to the hut and its contents was estimated at £1,250 so a public appeal was launched to replace both. In the meantime, another village Scout troop offered the 1st Thatcham Scouts temporary use of its facilities. However, Ray Frankland remained leader of 1st Thatcham until 1983, by which time it comprised two Scout troops (Dartmoor and Exmoor) and two Cub packs.

Another troop had been formed in Thatcham back in 1955 – the 2nd Thatcham Scout Group. It was an 'open' group, intended to complement the 1st Thatcham troop, whose members had to be Church of England. Its group Scoutmaster was Mr Frederick Mien of Bath Road. The Scoutmaster was Mr Ray Rogers, assisted by Mr George Brown and the Cubmaster was Sapper Douglas Bell, of Denison Barracks, Hermitage, assisted by Miss Margaret Looker of Bath Road.

In 1966 this troop had 'Greenham Court' added to its name in tribute to Major Bostock, who had helped to set up the group and who lived at Greenham Court, Newbury. From its early days, the troop had also met in a wooden ex-army hut, located at the Memorial Playing Fields. However, a new purpose-built headquarters was erected here for them (and shared with the local Bowls Club), being opened for use in February, 1979.

For ten years from 1987 Barry Wilson was Scout leader of the 1st Thatcham and it was in his time that their present Scout hut was constructed at the Church Gate site. The new brick hut, part prefabri-

Mr Tony Taylor of Loverock Construction is rewarded by Thatcham Girl Guides for contributing £100 towards a new Scout and Guide hut in November 1972.

The 1st Thatcham Scouts march up the Broadway as part of the Remembrance Day parade in November 1991.

Above: *Thatcham Girl Guide, Jennifer Smith, helping members of a Brownie pack in about 1974.*

Right: *Thatcham Girl Guides on a camp at Chamberhouse Farm in about 1967.*

Twin sisters, Katherine and Joanne Ballard, are presented with their Queen's Guide awards – the first ever twins in the 2nd Thatcham guides to achieve this distinction – in December 1979.

opened in 1981. This is a non-uniformed branch of Guiding open to anyone who was a Guide or Brownie, ex-Guiders who for various reasons are unable to run a unit, or anyone who has not made the Guide or Scout promise but subscribes to the aims and principles of the two Associations. For girls aged 5–7 Rainbows were started 1989.

Over the years the uniform and programme have changed with the times. Camping, outdoor pursuits and service to others are still a very strong part of the programme but there is more flexibility and the girls plan their own programme to reflect a modern lifestyle. Today, Guiding in Thatcham is thriving with one Ranger unit, four Guide companies, eight Brownie packs, three Rainbow units and one Trefoil Guild.

Thatcham Ladies Get Organised

Women in Thatcham have played a large part in its history in modern times, most notably through two particular organisations – the Women's Voluntary Service and the Women's Institute – which both established local branches just before the Second World War.

The Women's Voluntary Service was set up at this time and dedicated itself to helping win the war. Established by Lady Reading in May 1938, the first members were ladies recruited from her address book. By August 1939, the WVS had 336,000 members nationwide and almost a million by 1941. Thatcham's WVS branch started in the summer of 1939 with about 30 members.

Among the many jobs undertaken by Thatcham's WVS were billeting and welfare of evacuees, provision of school meals, running a mothers' club and different hostels – for bombed out mothers and children, Dagenham boys and Admiralty men. In the face of problems no-one else could cope with, the solution always seemed to be 'Ask the WVS'.

The ladies of the local WVS branch knitted for the forces, sent food parcels, did clerical work connected with ration books and fire watchers' registration. They also 'adopted' a corvette, ran book drives, collected rose hips and distributed vitamins for Thatcham children. They assisted at every fête, flag day and entertainment held in the village.

By far the most important work the Thatcham WVS branch did was salvage work. This began in July, 1940, after Lady Reading broadcast an appeal on behalf of the government to turn 'saucepans into Spitfires'. Scrap metal, rubber, rags, paper and bones were all collected and stored in a wooden WVS hut in Thatcham Broadway.

The materials were collected by the ladies themselves in cars, on bicycles – even in prams – and cleared weekly by lorry. Thatcham's WVS raised a total of £1,663.5s.11d. in this way by the end of the

cated by Guildway Buildings, was opened on 29 November 1986 – it consists of a main hall that can be divided into two smaller halls for more flexible use. It now affords excellent facilities for the boys in Thatcham's Scouts, Cubs and Beavers, along with the girls in the town's Guides and Brownies.

The village's girls were first catered for when a Brownie pack for 7–11 year olds was formed in Thatcham in May 1919. It was registered the following year as the 3rd Kennet Valley Brownies and re-registered as the 1st Thatcham pack in July 1927. Miss J.E.B. (Millicent) Turner was the first Brown Owl. She went on to become the local Girl Guides' Captain and the company often met at her family home, Thatcham House – the first record of Thatcham Guides is in 1928.

Another Brownie pack was formed in 1939 but disbanded in 1945. Other members of well-known families connected with local Guides and Brownies included Miss Henry and Miss Wallis. Over the years both Brownies and Guides progressed steadily with packs and companies fluctuating with the population and the availability of adults prepared to be leaders. From 1949 Miss Olive Blissett, who lived in Dunstan Green, ran 1st Thatcham Guides. They met at the Band Room in Green Lane.

The big event of that year was a county rally in Coley Park, Reading, in the presence of the Princess Royal. The Division Standard was carried by June O'Dell (now Milsom), from 1st Thatcham Guides. They also camped at Sidmouth, Devon, and had a day sightseeing in Exeter. The highlight of the week was being taken to the beach at night and being allowed to skinny dip!

A Ranger unit was started for girls aged 15 plus in 1977, but closed sometime in the 1980s as girls moved away or were old enough to be leaders themselves. (It has been restarted today.) A Trefoil Guild was

In 1955 members of the WVS from the Thatcham based Food Flying Squad attended an exercise with their water tank sterilisation vehicle – here they are seen tasting the water.

In 1953 the ladies of the Ministry of Food Flying Squad Column based at Thatcham, attended an exercise at Portsmouth in which they provided 900 meals for Civil Defence personnel.

The Thatcham based Food Flying Squad of the WVS had a 500 gal. water tanker and four canteen vans – the only lady who can be identified by name here is Mrs Doris Bridge, second right.

war. This was mostly given away to war charities, such as £104 to Thatcham Hospital Supplies, £86 for POW parcels and £35 to Earl Haig's Fund (Royal British Legion).

Funds were spent as fast as they were raised. Under a WVS gift scheme, servicemen and women were sent packs of cigarettes monthly – a total of 3,600 packs at a total cost of £500. The War Savings Group collected the sum of £1,451.19s.6d. during the war years. Thatcham's WVS also gave £80 to the village's War Memorial Fund.

However, as a WI branch was also established in the village before the war, membership of the local WVS actually dwindled during the war years – it only had 15 members by the end of the war, eight of whom were original members who had been present at the branch's first meeting six years earlier. When victory was declared in May 1945, American servicemen from Greenham Common – in celebratory spirit – set light to their salvage hut in the Broadway!

Having done some sterling war work, a Thatcham based WVS Food Flying Squad – of four canteen vans and a water tanker – continued to provide support at Civil Defence exercises across the region in the postwar years, being ready to cover any disaster that might arise. The ladies of the squad met fortnightly at Thatcham's Drill Hall for training – Mrs F Smith of Thatcham then played a prominent role. A local WRVS (as it is now known) branch remains active today.

Thatcham's WI was formed in October 1938. Its first meeting was attended by 90 local ladies who elected Mrs Cooke as President and Mrs Constance

Five members of Thatcham WI cut the 60th anniversary cake in 1998. Left to right: Mrs Janet Chapman (treasurer), Miss Iris Matthews (secretary), Mrs Margaret Craggs (who made the cake), Mrs Anne Davis (vice-president), Mrs Denise Cochrane (the oldest serving member, whose mother was a founding member in 1938).

Gilbert as Secretary. When war broke out less than a year later, the government requested help from the WI movement to prevent fruit going to waste. A network of 5,800 Preservation Centres was established and some 500 canning machines were supplied by the United States.

One machine came to Thatcham, where vast quantities of fruit were preserved in this way. Local WI members also picked rosehips from the hedgerows to help the war effort. They linked up with Ontario in Canada, from where onion, tomato and other seeds were sent to be grown in Thatcham. Seed potatoes were bought by members, who held an annual potato competition – the resulting crop was sent to the Cold Ash children's hospital.

Ladies of Thatcham WI present a bench to the parish c.1965. Left to right: Mrs Marshall, Mrs Hill, Mrs Sugden, Mrs Hardy, Mrs Grant, Mrs Cramb, Mrs Stradling, Mrs Kilberry.

Thatcham WI members attend an American Supper at Monks' Chambers, the home of their president in July 1976. Left to right: Mrs Head, Mrs Franklin, Mrs Cochrane (president), Mrs Hiscock.

Thatcham WI organised a Keep Thatcham Tidy campaign in summer 1982 – here, WI member Mrs Pauline Gresswell leads members' children on a clean up of the Broadway.

From 1942, when the Ministry of Supply started its salvage drive, members of the local WI got involved in rubber reclamation by making soft slippers from old tyres! The WI also ran a soldiers' canteen at the Parish Hall, knitted garments for merchant seamen and made up clothing parcels for bomb victims. The WI helped with the reception of evacuee children and passed a resolution on the bad conditions in a school used for them in 1944.

After the war Thatcham's WI involved itself in more usual activities, although it did pass another resolution requesting a policeman to deal with the increased traffic on the road through the village in 1949. Before the war members of its embroidery classes had mooted the idea of a branch banner but this had to wait until 1949, when a sub-committee under Mrs Shaw (then President) chose a design incorporating the Thatched Cottages, a well-known local landmark, to go on it.

In November 1952, founder Secretary Mrs Gilbert presented the branch with a piece of real linen and Miss Mecey – an expert embroiderer – began the stitching, which was continued by a working party later. Dedication day was 8 September 1955, and Mrs Shaw – who had left Thatcham – came back to for the presentation of the branch banner to the President, Mrs Bower, at the Parish Hall. It was carried by standard-bearer Mrs Creed to the singing of 'Jerusalem'.

Thatcham WI's other interests include rambling and drama. The first award in its history was a certificate presented for the drama group's performance of *Anti-clockwise* at the 1952 WI Drama Festival. Play readings and individual recitals often featured at early branch meetings.

Performances were put on at Crown Court old people's home in Thatcham and at Fair Close Day Centre, Newbury. The rambling group dated back to the branch's early days.

In the autumn of 1975 over 200 WI members met at the Kennet School for the Kennet Valley group handicraft exhibition. As the host institution, Thatcham was responsible for entertaining the other seven institutes in the group. There were over 150 pieces of handiwork on show – Mrs Denise Cochrane, host President, exhibited several examples of her own handiwork, including some dainty bobbin lace.

In 1978 Thatcham WI celebrated its 40th anniversary with a dinner, at which founder Secretary Mrs Gilbert was a special guest. In November 1980 members planted six rose trees at Crown Court to celebrate the Queen Mother's birthday. In the summer of 1982 the branch organised parties of volunteers to tidy up the centre of Thatcham – the Keep Britain Tidy group provided plastic jackets and litter pickers for all those taking part. At time of writing the branch remains active.

Bringing Panto to the People of Thatcham

The origins of amateur theatricals in Thatcham can be traced back to the period following the First World War, when a group called 'Ye Ancient Britons' was established. It mainly comprised ex-scholars of the village's British and Council schools, who initially made a name for themselves in the early spring of 1924 by staging an operetta entitled 'Sherwood's Queen'. It was an entirely new venture but it proved a great success.

'Never before had there been an opportunity to witness such a properly produced operetta in the village performed by the inhabitants', we are told. 'Without doubt talent abounds in Thatcham, but the work of bringing these talents to the fore has never before been accomplished in this direction'. The production appealed to village residents of an artistic

The full cast of TAVA's 1946 pantomime Dick Whittington.   (ALL TAVA PHOTOGRAPHS COURTESY OF MRS J. HAWKINS)

Thatcham Amateur Variety Artistes' pantomime at the British School, January 1954. An annual event, the production on this occasion was Aladdin.

The full cast of TAVA's 1952 pantomime Babes in the Wood. *Valerie Hawkins and Peggy Slade were the 'babes'.*

The principal performers in TAVA's 1954 pantomime Aladdin. *The lead role was played by Barbara Gough, with Sheila Powell as the princess.*

The full cast of TAVA's 1955 pantomime Mother Goose.

The principal performers in TAVA's 1957 pantomime Robin Hood.

The full cast of TAVA's 1958 pantomime Jack and the Beanstalk.

The principal performers in TAVA's 1959 pantomime Robinson Crusoe.

temperament, being much appreciated by 'lovers of music and pretty stage scenes'.

The 'Ancient Britons' practiced weekly for up to eight months to perfect their shows. They were led by the local family of saddlers, the Ashmans – Sidney was the Honorary Secretary, with wife Anna (née Munro, who had come to the village as a suffragette some years earlier) and brother Frank playing leading roles. Their musical director was Miss Kate Carter. The group staged shows regularly during the 1920s and 1930s.

However, a village drama society with a tradition of pantomime productions was set up immediately after the Second World War and was known as the 'Thatcham Amateur Variety Artistes' (TAVA). Many members were local ex-servicemen who joined its ranks upon demob, such as John Eggleton, who heard about TAVA in a letter whilst still serving abroad with the army and paid 2s.6d. to join after returning home in 1949!

TAVA put on its first pantomime – *Babes in the Wood* – at the old Drill Hall in Thatcham Broadway on Boxing Day 1945, plus a series of matinee and evening shows through to Saturday 29 December. The group's original organiser was Harry Stevens, who wrote and produced the show as well as playing the role of Dame Trott. The 'babes' were played by Leoni Le Coq and Avis Brown, with Pat Breach as the Fairy Queen.

Harry Stevens was the production's general manager, with Bert Goble as stage manager and Will Fitch as the pianist. The cast was made up of local people whose names would be recalled by many today, with speciality acts from Doris Walker (vocalist) and Ernie Adams (comedian). Child dancers 'The Broadway Juveniles' came from Newbury's Broadway School of Dancing, with lighting and effects installed by Percy Kidd.

Also in the cast that year was Ted Gall, playing 'Cecil' (one of two robbers), who eventually took over from Harry Stevens as writer and producer. Ted had been born at Girvan, Scotland, in 1910 but had moved to Thatcham in 1934 to work at Reeds Corrugated Cases. He had assumed the mantle of writer and producer by 1948, when *Cinderella* was TAVA's Christmas offering.

In 1949, *Dick Whittington* was staged from 27–31 December inclusive. In true pantomime tradition, the lead role of Dick starred Molly Wood, with Ernie Steer as his cat! John Eggleton was the Bosun's Mate whilst his pal Arthur Smith played Idle Jack. By this date, Ted Gall was also TAVA's stage director but its general manager was Ralph Bell and its stage manager was Alf Tigwell.

There was a separate stage manager for the village's venue (the Drill Hall) in the person of George Barker, who ran a removal company at 19 Station Road and appropriately enough helped with scenery changes. The scenery was devised and painted by Trevor Gaunt & Co. and the 'ship' by Reg Pearce & Co.

TAVA staged *Jack and the Beanstalk*, with Ralph Bell as Jack's mother, in the new year of 1951 but this was the last time it used the Drill Hall as its venue. From the new year of 1952, TAVA switched its productions to the British School in Church Lane, where it put on *Babes in the Wood* again – this time, though, Valerie Hawkins and Peggy Slade played the 'babes'. John Eggleton and Arthur Smith featured as robbers.

And so the pantomime favourites continued year on year, as TAVA staged its annual shows for the villagers of Thatcham. For coronation year, the 1953 production was *Cinderella* again, with Sheila Powell starring as the principal girl. Its January 1954, production was *Aladdin*, with Barbara Gough in the star role and Sheila Powell as the princess. In January 1955, TAVA put on *Mother Goose* with Ben Williams in the leading role. John Eggleton doubled as her friend Mrs Brown and (along with Trevor Gaunt) as the comedy horse!

The list goes on: in 1957, from 14–19 January inclusive, TAVA presented the village with its own version of *Red Riding Hood*. This time the lead role was taken by Jill Milford, with John Eggleton as the squire. Ben Williams was *Mother Hubbard* and by now was the producer too. Ted Gall still wrote the script and played the Wolf.

TAVA's 1958 production, from 10–15 February inclusive, was *Jack and the Beanstalk*, with Rhoda Taylor as Jack and Stan Wright as his mother, Dame Trott. The Giant was played by Peter Tosdevine. Ben Williams and Ted Gall were again producer and scriptwriter respectively. *Robinson Crusoe* was staged from 12–17 January inclusive in 1959, with Shirley Andrews as principal girl and Pam Jolly as principal boy; but this proved to be TAVA's last pantomime and thereafter the group disbanded.

Thatcham Amateur Variety Artistes had brought pantomime to the village for 15 years. Ted Gall, who retired from Reeds in 1977 and died aged 76 in February 1987, had written all their scripts since 1948. In this way, as well as entertaining the villagers, he had helped the thespians of postwar Thatcham to find an outlet for their talents.

Founder member of TAVA seen at his place of work, Reeds Corrugated Cases (Colthrop), in 1951.

A KATS show with a difference – a performance of This, That and the Other *in 1978 featuring Tony Jones in massive chaps!*

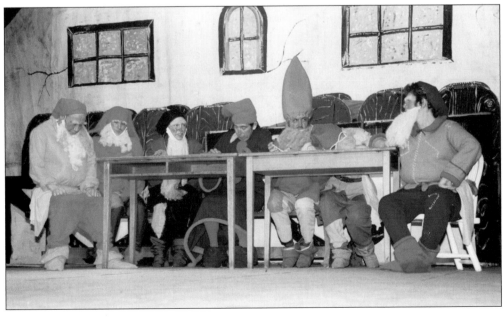

KATS Christmas pantomime in 1983, Snow White and the Seven Dwarfs.

KATS Christmas pantomime in 1980, Mother Goose *with Tony Jones as the Dame.*

KATS Christmas pantomime in 1973, Little Red Riding Hood.

KATS Christmas pantomime in 1985, Aladdin *featuring Widow Twankey with Wishy Washy and Aladdin himself.*

KATS: Theatre for Thatcham

Kennet Amateur Theatrical Society (KATS) was set up by the Kennet School PTA in 1968. Their intention was to produce light hearted plays once or twice a year. They staged their first production – William Morum and William Dinner's comedy thriller, *Too Soon For Daisies* – at Kennet School in 1969. At this date, the group consisted of only about a dozen members led by Betty Cole – a very energetic and determined lady.

After the success of this first production, ambitions grew and the pantomime *Little Miss Muffet*, along with an *Old Tyme Music Hall* review, were both presented in 1971. The group had now found its niche – appealing to the theatre goers of the growing town of Thatcham and providing more light-hearted fare than Newbury's Operatic Society.

By the early 1970s, a production pattern had been established, with a light-hearted play delivered in the spring (often a farce), a musical review in the autumn and a traditional pantomime over the Christmas season. Membership grew steadily and was soon up to almost 40. Betty Cole's hard work was continued by a number of stalwarts including Musical Director, Martin Eggleton (still a member today) and Mick and Sandra Tucker.

Sue and Trevor Dobson were heavily involved in the design and production of ever more ambitious plays and reviews. One aspect that set the group apart was the fact that everything they used was home made (both sets and costumes) and for many years Trevor's mother, Eileen Dobson, created lavish costumes for chorus lines that could exceed 30 performers. That meant 15 gowns for the women and 15 suits for the men – a true labour of love!

This pattern of three productions per year continued into the mid-1990s. KATS' performances included Noel Coward's *Blithe Spirit*, Richard Harris's *Outside Edge* and Jeffrey Archer's *Beyond Reasonable Doubt*, as well as three 'Old Tyme Music Halls' and a wide range of traditional pantomimes such as *Cinderella* and *Pinocchio*. There were also performances of *The Wizard of Oz* and a sequel written solely for the theatre, *Return to the Land of Oz*.

Whilst Newbury's Corn Exchange was closed in the 1980s and early 1990s, KATS became the only theatrical group to perform a seasonal pantomime. Many grown-ups living in the locality today gained their earliest experience of the theatre by attending a KATS panto!

In 1999 the group performed Terry Pratchett's *Wyrd Sisters* – specially adapted for the stage from this author's popular book. In Pratchett's work, the group had found a new audience and followers of his fantastic stories attended from as far away as Holland and Canada.

Such was the success of this production that the group has since followed up with two more of his

works – *Carpe Jugulum* in 2001 and *The Truth* in 2005. In fact, Terry Pratchett attended *Carpe Jugulum* and declared himself satisfied that the group had done it justice!

Today, KATS is a thriving group of over 50 members under the chairmanship of Trevor Eggleton (a member of over 30 years' standing), supported by many selfless individuals such as Mike and Mandy Cole and Claire Helyer. Its productions have earned the group a superb reputation in the Newbury and Thatcham District.

KATS also takes part in many community activities, including the annual Christmas lights ceremony in Thatcham Broadway and the Thatcham Festival of Arts. Musical review has given way to published musicals including *Oliver* and *Little Shop of Horrors* but a traditional pantomime is still performed each February to full houses and critical acclaim.

The Festival Spirit in Old Thatcham

In 1970 the residents of Thatcham entered into the spirit of things when they enjoyed a nine-day Folk Festival during late June/early July. The festival featured a variety of events in and around the village green and was probably both the first and the last time such an ambitious programme was staged here in the twentieth century!

The festival ran from a Saturday to the following Sunday week and things literally started with a bang on the first morning by an anvil salute that was fired in the Broadway. Organised by Mr Laurie Turner (head of St Mary's School), and witnessed by an audience of thousands, there was an interesting variation on the traditional firing method.

In days gone by gunpowder was used to fire the anvils but on this occasion it was replaced by an explosive substance used in the jet industry. A quadruple explosion was set up and ignited, sending four loud reports echoing around the Broadway. The last occasion when anvils had been fired was the coronation in 1953 and it has never been done since.

Speeches were made by local dignitaries. Mr B.G. Merriman, the chairman of Thatcham Parish Council, paid tribute to the hard work carried out by the festival committee. Its chairman, Mr George Hurford (head of Kennet School), reminded parishioners that six centuries earlier Thatcham had been one of the most important places in Berkshire.

Next, pupils from St Mary's and Francis Baily schools gave a display of country dancing to the accompaniment of their own musical instruments. The Kennet School brass band played selections, then both the Boys' and Girls' Brigade bands played whilst giving an impressive marching display. A mobile exhibition was opened at St Mary's Church.

This featured pottery, needlework, collage and paintings. Indeed, one picture – an elongated nude

Francis Baily Primary School pupils perform three dances accompanied by recorders and percussion instruments.

Pupils from St Mary's and Francis Baily Primary Schools perform folk dances on the green.

study of a woman – prompted one visitor to complain that it was obscene but his request that it be removed was not acted upon. (An exhibition staged by a children's playgroup at St Mary's Hall in the Broadway proved to be much less controversial!)

A flower festival was put on at St Mary's Church, on the theme 'From the Cradle to the Grave'. There was baptism at the font, confirmation at the chapel screen, communion at the altar, marriage at the Danvers' tomb and the commendation of the dying at the war memorial. The bell ringers had put on an exhibition including plaques and photographs.

On that first Saturday evening the festivities continued with a square dance at Harts Hill Farm, the home of Mr and Mrs John Simmons. Here two large barns accommodated the 300 dancers who were 'called' by Mr Albert Moss. So ended the first busy day of the festival – but there were eight more to come and the Sunday was devoted to religion.

St Mary's Church was packed on Sunday evening for a recorded half-hour BBC *Songs of Praise* service. A 200-strong choir recruited from local churches and schools combined to produce singing of 'volume and quality'. Mr Richard Sargeantson (the Kennet School's head of music) conducted the choir whilst the Revd Stanley Cornish led the prayers.

The musical theme continued on the Monday evening, but in a more secular vein, at St Mary's School. Again, local choirs combined to produce a varied programme. The Kennet School choir and staff opened the proceedings with a selection of songs including a lively arrangement of 'Liza Jane' which got them an encore from the audience.

Next, a piano duet by Alan and Anne Kingston created a whirlwind of sound with 'Tourbillon' by Melan-Gueroult. Another of the highlights of the show was a performance by the Thatcham Old Folks choir. Mostly in their seventies, the choir managed an enthusiastic selection including the 'Neapolitan Boat Song' and 'Red River Valley'.

Another encore was earned by Raymond Aitken for his rendition of Handel's 'Silent Worship' whilst young Anne Hawkins showed great versatility, first playing the violin and then the guitar. St Mary's Church choir sang the negro spiritual 'Steal Away', and Mr V. Stratton (accompanied by his wife) sang Vaughan Williams' songs impeccably.

A note of humour was introduced by Thatcham Congregational and Methodist Church choirs with 'The Goslings' and their young people's choir was well-received. The Girls' Brigade played recorders and the evening concluded with the combined choirs' performance of the Rodgers and Hammerstein number 'It's a Grand Night for Singing'!

Thatcham's nine-day Folk festival continued into early July. The musical events of the first three days continued, along with others based on such activities as dancing and sport. The organisers seemed to have thought of everything and to have provided entertainment for every imaginable taste – as was evidenced later in the week.

On Tuesday, an evening of light entertainment was staged at the British School. Pauline Wootton and Tracey Walker, two seven year olds, gave a dancing display and there was ballet dancing too from Pauline Hunt and Susan Morse. Miss Dorothy Bradford recited amusing monologues and Maurice Sloan sang some old-time songs.

A golf course sketch featuring Robert Joyce and Arthur Smith was well received. Ronald Baker played the trumpet, then there was rapturous applause for Anthony Lavelle and Gina, a Newbury Grammar School magician and assistant. Newbury Symphony Orchestra lead violin Felicity Salter played and Alec Jenkins sang folk songs.

The highlight of the evening was Thatcham's Bluebell Girls performing the cancan in a line-up that included a couple of men as well as some of the village matrons! The producer of this event was Mr David Wootton. Other Tuesday events were an afternoon concert at Francis Baily School plus a jazz evening at the Kennet School.

Francis Baily School also hosted a fashion show on Wednesday. Kennet School pupils modelled outfits they had made at school or in their leisure time – the items ranging from bikinis to evening wear!

Jeff Neal (metalwork teacher at Kennet School) steps forward to fire a 'salute' of four anvils.

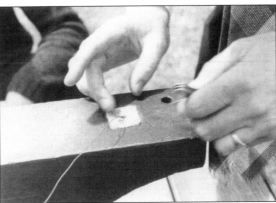

Above: *A close-up view showing how gunpowder and fuse were used to prime an anvil for firing.*

Left: *Jeff Neal* (left) *and Laurie Turner* (right) *get their heads together in the delicate task of priming.*

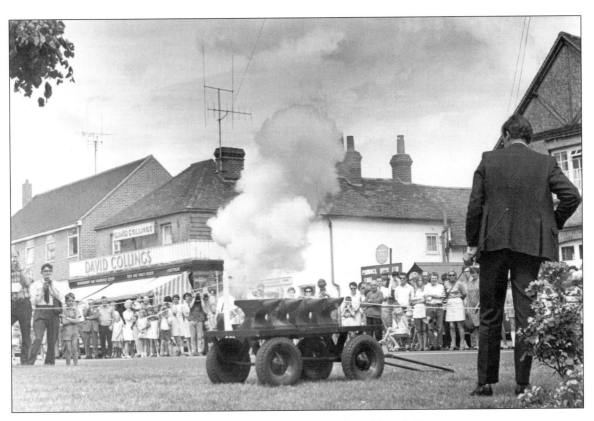

The last anvil salute ever fired in Thatcham, by Jeff Neal (right) *and Laurie Turner.*

A display was given by members of the Thatcham Evening Institute classes, some of whom modelled alongside their young daughters.

One slightly disappointing aspect of the festival was the poor attendance at Thursday afternoon's concert of choral and instrumental music at the Kennet School. A pity really, as the programme was varied, with vocals, recorders, brass band and orchestra (conducted by Mr Richard Sargeantson), plus excerpts from the musical *Oliver*.

On Friday evening, two local primary schools – St Mary's and Francis Baily – combined to stage a concert arising from their year's course work, featuring both choral and instrumental items. At the Kennet School, five local groups – The Final Decision, Last Night Confession, Sobranie Sound, The Baron and The Burlesque – played 'pop'.

The weekend was very busy with capacity audiences at most events – some folk had to be turned away from certain venues. The Kennet School was crowded for what was the climax of the week. St Mary's, Francis Baily and the Kennet Schools began the proceedings with a display of massed folk dancing featuring over 100 pupils.

In the school's swimming pool, Kennet Valley Canoe Club gave a display that included canoe rolling whilst on the field Kennet Youth Club members gave an archery display. Thatcham's Army Cadet Corps staged a realistic mock battle featuring a camouflaged truck. Visitors were treated to a fusillade of miniature explosions and gunfire.

Other activities included five-a-side football, swimming and life saving, acrobatics and a spectacular trampoline display by Kennet schoolboys, in the course of which some of the boys successfully somersaulted over the tops of two cars. Kennet pupils staged a dance-drama and local Girl Guides contributed some of their own activities.

As if that was not enough, there was a display of American Indian dances by Greenham Airbase Boy Scouts – clad in traditional costume – and a display of musketry drill and duelling by the Society of Cavaliers (who also featured in an evening performance of 'Merrie England'). Outdoor events ended with Army Cadets 'beating the retreat'.

The festival concluded next day when the Anglican and Congregational church choirs combined for a service of thanksgiving at the Congregational Church. Its minister, Revd Frederick Spriggs, conducted the service and an address was given by Revd Stanley Cornish of St Mary's Church. Festival chairman Mr George Hurford read lessons.

'A lot of hard work has been given by a lot of people', said Mr Hurford, 'but the final result has made it all worthwhile'. The cost of staging the nine-day festival was estimated at £800 but attendances at most of the events were so good that the organisers expected not only to cover their costs but to make a small profit for worthy causes. For the new millennium, Thatcham's town council inaugurated its own annual nine-day Autumn Festival of Arts and Leisure in 2001, but the village's Folk Festival in 1970 was a worthy forerunner.

Subscribers

Gareth and Sharon Adams, Lower Way, Thatcham, Berkshire
Graham J. Aedy, Thatcham, Berkshire
Jean Atkinson (née Adams), Cold Ash
Christopher B. Ball, Thatcham, Berkshire
Kenneth Gordon Beabey-Roberts
Colin F. Benham, Cold Ash, Berkshire
Anne T. Bergin, Thatcham, Berkshire
Wilfred and Sheila Bint, Thatcham
William G. Black, Thatcham, Berkshire
Mr and Mrs F. Bridger
Jeffrey and Marilyn Britt, Thatcham
Jeff Brooks, Thatcham
Philip A. Brownlie, Thatcham, Berkshire
Ruth E.A. Burge, Thatcham, Berkshire
Maureen Butcher, Thatcham, Berkshire
Richard Butler, St Albans
Dave Carter, Thatcham, Berkshire
Dorothy Chapman, Thatcham, Berkshire
Derek Roy Chivers
Denise M. Cochrane (née Brown), Thatcham, Berkshire
John Collins, Ashmore Green
Mr Clive Cook and Family, Old Briar Cottage, Ashford Hill
Mr David Cooper, Thatcham, born and bred
Mr Keith Cooper, Newbury, born in Thatcham
Linda Craig, Fraserburgh, Aberdeenshire
Marjorie J. Davidson, Thatcham, Berkshire
Mrs Susan P. Dean, Thatcham, Berkshire
Stewart Dempster
Sue Dillon, Thatcham, Berkshire
Pauline M. Doughty, New Malden, Surrey
Mr and Mrs P. Dowd
Douglas Durbidge, Welwyn Garden City, Hertfordshire
Ronald A. Durbidge, Thatcham, Berkshire
Nathan and Prisana Emerson, Thatcham
Jeremy Fisher, Thatcham, Berkshire
Howard, Elaine and Will Fletcher, Thatcham
Tom Fletcher, New Zealand
Pat and Ray Foan, Shelley Road, Thatcham, Berkshire
Margaret Ina Ford, Thatcham, Berkshire
Mr Ray Freemantle
Cliff W. Fry, Newbury
Tony Gale, Thatcham
Ted Gall (in memory of)
Monica J. Gildersleeves, Thatcham, Berkshire
Lionel Haines, Thatcham, Berkshire
Michael Haines, Thatcham
Mrs Valerie Hawkins-Gallagher, Yorktown, Va, USA
Kevin and Veronica Heimsoth, Thatcham, Berkshire
Vicki I. Herlingshaw, Thatcham, Berkshire
Roy P. Hill, Thatcham, Berkshire
Sheila C. Hill, Thatcham, Berkshire
Olive Hiscock (née Matthews), Northfield Road, Thatcham
Mr and Mrs S. Hollingbery, Thatcham, Berkshire
David R.G. Honey, Thatcham, Berkshire
Leonard (Podge) Hunt, Thatcham
Margaret H. Huntley, Thatcham, Berkshire
Edith M. Hutchings, Thatcham, Berkshire

John and Penny Hutchings, Thatcham, Berkshire
Nigel D. Hutchings, Thatcham, Berkshire
P. Hutchings, Thatcham, Berkshire
Jason M.R. Hutt, Snowdon Close, Thatcham, Berkshire
Nancy and Roy Hutt, Thatcham
Sue and Ritchie Hutt, Thatcham
Charles Henry Hyde, Thatcham, Berkshire
Paul and Niki Hyde, Paynesdown Road, Thatcham, Berkshire
Kennet School, Thatcham, Berkshire
Deborah A. Kennett, Wokingham, Berkshire
R. and M. King, Thatcham
Mr Michael H.C. Lamden, Thatcham, Berkshire
Alison M. Laughton, Thatcham, Berkshire
Thomas J. Lees, Thatcham, Berkshire
Keith E. Lewis, Yattendon, Berkshire
The Lewis Family, Bath Road, Thatcham
Jane Lock, Chamberhouse Mill Lane
Beverley Lyford, Thatcham, Berkshire
Malcolm K. Macdonald and Sheila Macdonald (née Broughton), Thatcham, Berkshire
Iris Matthews, born (and still living at) Northfield Road, Thatcham
Mr and Mrs R.J.S. Miles, Thatcham, Berkshire
Mrs Janet Miller, Thatcham, Berkshire
The Mulliner Family, Thatcham
Violet E. Mussett, Thatcham, Berkshire
James Nicholls, Bucklebury, Berkshire
Beryl North (née Spriggs), Thatcham
A. Northway
David Norton, Thatcham, Berkshire
Helen O'Leary, Thatcham, Berkshire
Parsons Down Junior School, Thatcham, Berkshire
Kenneth I. Paulin, Thatcham, Berkshire
Patricia A. Powell, Thatcham, Berkshire
Douglas and Evelyn Richardson, Thatcham
Amanda J. Scade, Thatcham
Alfred E. Shadlock, Donnington
Mr and Mrs R. Skelly, Thatcham, Berkshire
Mrs N. Soper, Thatcham
Tony Stacey
Peter G. Stanbrook, Thatcham, Berkshire
Mr Pat Tanner, Newbury, Berkshire
Jolene J.I. Taylor
Peter C. Taylor, Thatcham, Berkshire
Ronald J. Taylor, Thatcham
Stephen J. Taylor, Thatcham
Tony Taylor, Thatcham
Pam Thompson, Thatcham, Berkshire
Sandy and Terry Thorpe, Thatcham
Victoria Sellwood Turner, Southampton
John F.W. Walling, Newton Abbot, Devon
Richard W. Wallington
Malcolm Warren, Paynesdown Road, Thatcham
Splash, Sara and Anna Waters, Thatcham, Berkshire
Eileen West (née Elliott), Thatcham
Malcolm E. Whale, Carrbridge, Inverness-shire
Maxine Whyborn, Thatcham, Berkshire
Adrian J. Wootton, Bath Road, Thatcham
David and Barbara Wootton, Chislet House, Thatcham
Stanley T. Wright, Thatcham, Berkshire
Nick Young, Thatcham, Berkshire

There are now over 160 titles in the Community History Series.
For a full listing of these and other Halsgrove publications,
please visit www.halsgrove.com or telephone 01884 243242.